SEARCH FOR MEANING
A faith exploration programme for 16-plus year-olds

TEACHER'S BOOK

Compiled by
Judith Russi SSMN

Illustrated by Arthur Baker

GEOFFREY
CHAPMAN

Geoffrey Chapman
An imprint of Cassell Publishers Ltd
Artillery House, Artillery Row, London SW1P 1RT, England

The worksheets featured in this book are available in a
separate publication (ISBN 0-225-66608-1)
which entitles the purchasing institution
to make unlimited copies of the designated contents.

First published 1990

British Library Cataloguing in Publication Data
Russi, Judith
    Search for meaning
    Teacher's book.
    1. Catholic adolescents. Christian life
    I. Title
    248.8'3

ISBN 0-225-66607-3

Typeset by Fons et Culmen
Printed and bound in Great Britain by
Biddles Ltd, Guildford and Kings Lynn

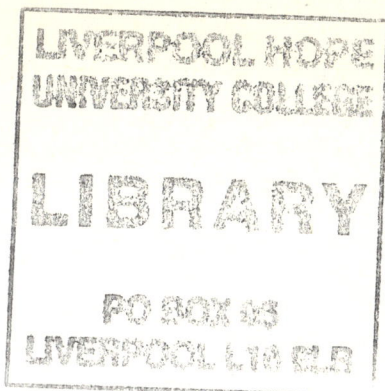

INTRODUCTION

WHO IS THE PROGRAMME FOR?

This programme is intended for young adults who have completed their fifth year of secondary schooling; but it is not exclusively for use in schools. It has been designed to form the basis for any 16-plus religious education programme. It can be used in non-Catholic parishes and schools as well as in Catholic parishes and schools.

USING THE PROGRAMME
IN NON-CATHOLIC SCHOOLS

The structure and content of the programme can be equally successful in non-Catholic schools, though careful thought and preparation may be needed to get the right input and to be sensitive to where the students are. Since this teacher's book is not in the students' hands there should be no problem about rephrasing the input suggested here as appropriate to each situation, or choosing different input material within the framework this book offers. In many of the units input from other faiths can also be used, and there may be students and staff who can contribute. In some sixth forms it may be more appropriate to open with the Unit on morality (Unit 1), rather than the Introductory Unit.

1

IN AND OUT OF FORMAL EDUCATION

Although this programme has been extensively piloted in schools and sixth form colleges, it has been designed so that it can be used in a parish-based setting, for example for young adults who have not opted for higher education, or who are attending colleges which do not offer any form of religious education or formation.

The purpose of this programme is to address the concerns of those working in religious education and the formation of young adults. It is written by teachers who have considerable experience of teaching religious education at this level, and reflects their successes - and failures! It is the product of their experience, addressing our shared anxieties and building on our shared hopes.

As such, *Search for Meaning* is not a definitive document: it is a series of shared thoughts and approaches rooted in a wide variety of experiences. The programme has been appraised and revised in the course of the piloting not only by those teaching, but also by the students themselves.

All too often, religious education at this level follows the traditional 'confessional approach'. This is characterized by the transmission of a series of rules, dogmas and beliefs offered as solutions to life, leading, if adopted, to a total lifestyle. This approach has a certain validity as a working aim, but it has to be said that it has not provoked a positive response from 16-plus students in general.

In our experience, we need an entirely different starting point. We must begin with the student as an individual: as a reflective being who has been formed by various factors, sociological, psychological, physiological; each student has had different and unique experiences which will have formed different outlooks on life.

One thing characterizes 16-plus students: whether they will admit it or not, they are all engaged in a search for meaning.

Now, as religious educators we deeply value what the Gospel has to offer each individual in terms of fulfilment and growth. Therefore, in what we do, there must be a balance between, on the one hand, individual students and their circumstances, and on the other hand, the structure of the Church within which we operate, and which offers the opportunity for growth within a communal and social context.

What we should be concerned about, therefore, are successful procedures, rather than successful results (especially since, as experience shows, we cannot guarantee the latter!).

The preoccupation with successful results is the main cause of our disappointment. Though we work on the rightful conviction that we have a set of valuable and well-defined criteria to be transmitted, these are often rejected by the students. If we are honest we will admit that we are all seekers and searchers, and that each of us, student and teacher, is at a different stage in our personal journey of discovery.

It is unfair to expect 16-plus year-olds to accept definitive answers to life's mysteries. We know that at different stages of our own lives we have responded in different ways. Our task, then, is not to offer ready-made answers, but rather to provide the framework for finding the answers in the context of the Gospel and its realization through the Church. We are all on a faith journey.

If there is evidence that because of or after a session, a student is thinking, this is as successful a result as we should look for. Without thought, there is no hope of acceptance. Just because we don't get a response that pleases us it doesn't mean that that response is not important. No response at all conveys a message.

Our experience shows that we must be honest and start where students are. We must accept that the starting point will not be the same for each student. The only way that progress can be made is through meaningful dialogue. Meaningful dialogue is honest dialogue. This means that there has to be a relationship of trust, openness and honesty between student and teacher/catechist. An essential ingredient in this is that both should be willing to share honestly about where they are on their faith journey. In other words, the teacher/catechist must not play the role of the source of all wisdom, but should admit that they too are seeking.

If we provoke what seems to be an ignorant response from the students, it may well be due to a confusion, rather than a lack of knowledge. This usually manifests itself in the seemingly conflicting views of the universe from the Bible and the world of science. It is a consequence of poor religious teaching

3

earlier in life, but can be overcome by effective teaching.

There isn't usually a reluctance to admit to being a believer or being religious; but many young people do not willingly see the need to express belief publicly.

There seems to be confusion, if not conflict, between private and public religion. A great deal of education is needed to lead young adults to realize and appreciate the balance between individual and social experience.

There is also a need to provide a framework within which concrete levels of understanding can be transformed into more abstract cognitive growth.

By tackling these areas of concern in a framework of openness, our aim is to lead students as they enter adulthood into constructive self-questioning of their beliefs and opinions; to provide a framework in which these beliefs, values and opinions can be tested against the message of the Gospel and within the context of the Church.

This programme has been designed to provide such a framework. We believe it is flexible enough to serve either as a useful starting point and resource collection, or as a more definitive guide, depending on the needs of your situation.

MAKING THE PROGRAMME WORK FOR YOU

PRE-PROGRAMME PREPARATION

Search for Meaning began as a result of undertaking an honest appraisal of how things stood in the area of religious education. The survey and appraisal was difficult, but our findings made it quite clear that we had to make a far greater commitment to religious education at the 16-plus level. This evaluation became the foundation for something much more exciting for both students and staff; it resulted in a programme that was to be the vehicle through which students and staff shared a considerable amount of time together in a joint 'search for meaning'.

If *Search for Meaning* is to be truly effective for you, there is a sense in which you should first undertake an appraisal of the place and priority you accord to religious education.

The following checklists may help you do this:

1. What provision is there for the religious education of your 16-plus students?
2. How much time is allocated to religious education?
3. Staffing: what discussion is there about suitable staff? Who is involved in these discussions? What is/should be the student:staff ratio?
4. Resources: how much financial support is there?
5. How seriously is religious education taken by the students and staff or leaders?
6. How suitable is your venue?

If you are planning to use *Search for Meaning* in a school/college situation, certain fundamental requirements must be met:

1. Religious education must be timetabled first. This should be protected time for the students.
2. Staff will need time for:
- pre-programme in-service;
- the opportunity for evaluation and discussion before the start of each new unit.
3. Staff will need to be aware that this programme is more than a 'slot of time';

- that it will involve both students and staff together in preparing 'inputs' for the input sessions, as well as preparations for the debates, planning the conferences, planning the celebrations, and co-ordinating the involvement with the local community.

4. Resources for each unit, and research materials for the debate topics, need to be easily accessible to both staff and students.

OVERCOMING OBSTACLES AND DIFFICULTIES

There are circumstances where there is little financial support, and few staff or leaders available. Can the programme still be implemented? The answer is yes. Obviously, you will have to adapt it to suit your situation:

- the leader/teacher notes are sufficient to carry out a session;
- ideally, the group work should be carried out in small groups, but it can, if necessary, be made to work where there is one leader to 35 students!
- think of using suitable students as group leaders. They can be trained as any other person would be to work with the programme;
- if for some reason your time allocation cannot be changed (though do not give in too easily on this!), then the input session can be at one time, and the discussion/activity session at another.

INVOLVING PARENTS, FRIENDS, GOVERNORS, CLERGY

If you find that you are the only member of staff available for 16-plus religious education, then invite a suitable parent, friend of the school, governor, or member of the clergy to come in and be part of the programme. They may be able to do no more than one unit with you; they may have more time to spare. Remember to share with them the leader/teacher notes: these will help guide and control the inputs, and may help to give confidence to your staff/leaders. It may encourage you to know that this is how the first draft of this programme began!

PRE-PROGRAMME INTRODUCTION

It is essential to take time to explain the process that underlies this programme before the introductory unit begins:

- the programme is divided into units;
- each unit consists of six sessions;
- five of these sessions are input/discussion sessions; the sixth session completes the unit with a debate on the theme or topic of the unit.
- each session will need a minimum of an hour, and we suggest a maximum of one and a half hours. However, this should be adapted to fit the needs and situation of the group.

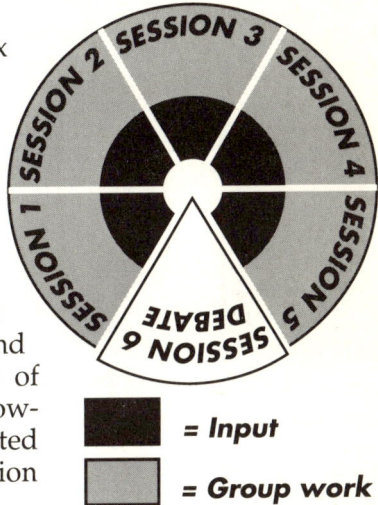

= Input

= Group work

WHAT FORM DOES THE INPUT TAKE?

The programme suggests a variety of input forms: mini-lecture; video; drama; testimony. Materials have been suggested, based on what has proved successful in the pilot schemes. We expect teachers and leaders to be able to add to what we offer, to make it topical by using current pop songs, current TV programmes, etc. There is room at the end of most of the sessions in this book for you to add your own notes of appropriate material. This input should last between 20 and 30 minutes.

WHAT HAPPENS FOR THE REST OF THE SESSION?

After the input those taking part in the programme move into small groups for the rest of the session. The Worksheets have been designed to stimulate the individual and small group work for this part of each session. There are two ways that this group work might be conducted. We will begin with the ideal model, where each student opts for the avenue along which he/she will proceed.

THE TWOFOLD AVENUE

The students are presented with the theme of the topic, and with two sets of statements (mini-posters of both of these sets of statements are available as copiable masters in the Worksheet book).

You will notice that this first poster's statements show a tendency towards an acceptance of faith, so we shall call this the 'critical faith acceptance avenue'.

> 'I believe in God and go to church.'
>
> 'Faith matters.'
>
> 'I'm interested, but may not get too involved.'
>
> 'Would call myself religious, even though I may not go to church.'
>
> 'I respect all religious belief.'

> 'I don't believe in God.'
>
> 'Religion is a waste of time.'
>
> 'I'm interested to know why people believe.'
>
> 'I respect religion, and want people to respect my views.'
>
> 'Most of the time, I just don't know what to think.'

The statements on this second poster show an uncertainty, an objective non-commitment attitude. We will call this the 'critical faith questioning' avenue.

WHICH OF THESE POSTERS BEST REFLECTS HOW YOU FEEL TODAY?

'I believe in God
and go to church.'

'Faith matters.'

'I'm interested,
but may not get too involved.'

'Would call myself religious,
even though I may not go to church.'

'I respect all religious belief.'

'I don't believe in God.'

'Religion is a waste of time.'

'I'm interested to know
why people believe.'

'I respect religion,
and want people to respect my views.'

'Most of the time, I just don't know
what to think.'

GROUP A

GROUP B

GROUP C

GROUP D

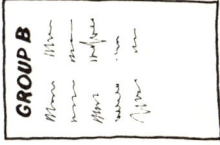
GROUP E

GROUP F

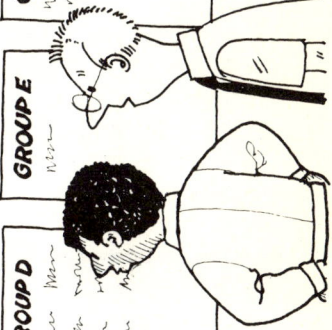

9

First, the group leaders should decide which avenue they feel comfortable with for the theme of the Unit.

The students are then invited to sign on for the small groups under either the 'critical faith acceptance avenue', or the 'critical faith questioning avenue', according to which best represents how they feel at the moment.

When the Introductory Unit has been completed the students should be encouraged to look at the posters again, and to rethink which avenue they would like to follow for the next Unit. It will depend on the theme or subject that the Unit covers whether each student prefers to stay in the same avenue, or whether the other avenue represents more appropriately how they feel now.

BOTH AVENUES ARE EQUALLY VALID

Notice it is *not* the case that one avenue is positive, whereas the other is negative. The statements have been chosen so that each avenue is represented by not only positive and negative statements, but also some 'grey' ones in between.

Nor is the student being invited to identify with all the statements on one or other of the posters. What is asked is that each student respond honestly, placing him/herself in the grouping that corresponds most closely to how he/she feels today. No student should feel they 'ought' to be in either group.

Similarly, in accepting to lead a group under one of the avenues, the group leaders must feel they are able to contribute sympathetically to the work of the group.

Above all, what is important is that both avenues should be 'critical': no matter which avenue is being followed, the students need to be challenged to think, to question, to evaluate.

SIZE AND SELECTION OF GROUPS

The smaller the groups, the better. This will depend on the number of teachers/group leaders available. Experience suggests eight students per group leader is the ideal ratio. But certainly, no group should exceed fifteen students.

AN EXAMPLE

Here is a schematic lay-out of how this might work in terms of the Introductory Unit (see also pages 20-21):

INTRODUCTORY UNIT

An exploration of belief

What is belief? In whom?
In what?
Concrete examples and lives.
What motivates these
individuals to behave like this?
Belief . . . Belonging . . .
What is 'Church'?

The critical faith
questioning group
will be raising
questions like:
what is in this
topic?
why does 'faith'
have meaning for
some and not for
others?
is there anything
that could replace
it effectively?

DEBATE

The Unit closes with
a general debate or
discussion involving
all the students and
staff/leaders.

The critical faith
acceptance group
will be raising
questions like:
How does my faith
compare with the
examples
explored?
What are the
implications of my
faith in my life?
Is it right to talk
about 'my' faith?

At the end of each unit the students will be free to re-select and form new groups that correspond to how they feel now. Ideally, the group leaders will find that students flow from one 'attitude' to the other as they develop.

This is in itself a learning opportunity for the students, a chance for them to discern more deeply how they feel about faith-related topics. For example, someone who begins in a faith acceptance avenue will come to recognize that there are some facets and features of his/her faith about which he/she has more questions than for others. Where appropriate, then, a student will follow some units with a faith questioning perspective, whilst other themes will be treated from the faith acceptance stance.

It may be necessary to spend some time clarifying the two approaches available to the student for each unit. Emphasize that:

- the students must choose freely;
- be careful of peer group pressure;
- whenever you sign up for one avenue, you stay with it for the rest of that unit. Only in exceptional circumstances should students be allowed to switch avenues in mid-unit.
- after the debate which draws each unit to a close, the students are then invited to look at the topic the next unit will cover. They then decide again which avenue to follow, according to the one that better represents how they feel now about this particular topic. Encourage the students to work out which avenue they should follow in terms of questions like 'Where am I now?' or 'From which standpoint do I want to explore this area?'

SECOND POSSIBLE STRUCTURE FOR THE PROGRAMME

Where there is only a small group following the programme and where there is only one teacher/group leader, it may prove impossible in practical terms to offer the twofold avenue group approach. This means that the students have to be allocated to a group irrespective of where they feel they are, and irrespective of their attitude to religion and faith.

In some situations, dividing the students into groups in this way, irrespective of their 'attitude', may be more desirable. However, it is very important that everyone taking part in the programme feels accepted, that everyone's opinions will be respected by the group as a whole, even if not always agreed with.

THE DEBATE

The sixth session in every unit is devoted to a debate on the theme of the unit.

This debate and discussion have been built into the programme deliberately, because they build up in the students skills which form an important part of adult life. Too many of our young people seem unable to express adequately how they feel about religion and their beliefs in general, and how they see and feel about their faith in particular.

PREPARING WITH GROUP LEADERS

All group leaders must meet with the programme leader before beginning the programme, and before the introduction of each new unit to ensure that everyone is satisfied with what is expected of them.

The hallmark of this programme should be a sensitivity to wherever the individual happens to be in their journey of self- and faith-discovery. This should be as true in regard to the leaders as to the students. At these preliminary meetings you have the opportunity to establish whether leaders prefer not to be involved in particular topics or in particular approaches to some topics, either because of where they feel they are currently in their own faith journey, or because of their teaching/leadership style. For example, some group leaders may be happy leading groups down the critical faith acceptance avenue, but not feel comfortable with the critical faith questioning stance. Respect this, and work to your leaders' strengths. But in all events, all the leaders must be made aware of what is expected of them, and should be thoroughly briefed on how the programme is structured, and how their contribution fits into it.

Be careful not to disclose the names of the leaders to the students before they have signed up for the discussion/activity groups, otherwise students may be unduly influenced in their choice of group.

SETTING UP AND PREPARING THE DEBATE

The debate concludes each unit.

> - it is important to give everyone concerned enough time to prepare for the debate.
> - introduce the debate topic about two weeks before the debate is due to take place.
> - don't let the opposing sides in the debate be staff v. students! Ensure a happy balance of students and staff in each team.
> - set a limit to the number of times that any individual (staff or student) is on a debating team. This means as many as possible have the opportunity to take part in the debates.
> - the final choice of the debate topic should be made through a vote open to all the students and staff.
> - ideally, the person who chairs the programme should be someone not involved in the running of the programme.
> - preparation of the arguments should take place outside each session time. If in school, then staff might join students in the common room to prepare.

When the debate is taken seriously by both staff and students, it generates a whole new level of enthusiasm for the programme as a whole. You will also find it raises interest in religious education outside class-time, involving colleagues who would normally never be involved. Of course, it does take more time, but the rewards of this extra commitment more than outweigh the extra effort.

THE UNITS

A whole range of units are offered in this programme (and other additional units may be published in the future). You will find that this book offers ten units for use over two years. There are three basic types of units:

INTRODUCTORY UNIT which is a foundation course, and therefore needs to be the first unit undertaken by any group.

CONCLUDING UNIT which has been designed to draw the threads of the whole course together. It focuses on the young people facing their decisions for life.

THEMATIC UNITS which may be followed in any order.

At this stage we offer eight such units, but others could be developed, and may be published in subsequent years. So the ten units you will find in this programme are:

INTRODUCTORY
UNIT   **WHAT IS BELIEF?**
In whom or what? Proof?
Concrete examples... Lives...
What motivates these individuals to behave
  like this?
Belief...   Belonging...
What is Church?

THEME 1   **MORALITY**
Who decides?
Who has the right?

THEME 2   **CALLED TO BE . . .?**
Marriage/family life
Problems...   Joys...   Sufferings...
What alternatives to marriage?

THEME 3   **CARING COMMUNITY**
When does 'caring' lead to 'Church'?
Communal expression of faith...
Celebration of communal values...

THEME 4   **JUSTICE AND PEACE**
'Prophets of our time'
Social teaching of the Church

THEME 5   **THE WORD**
Scripture: valid or invalid?
Power of God...   Reflection of God...
Issues

THEME 6   **NEED TO COMMUNICATE**
How and why we communicate
Prayer
Prayers and praying

THEME 7	**' - ISMS'**
	Humanism...
	Capitalism...
	Marxism...
	Communism...

THEME 8	**DIVIDED CHRISTIANITY -**
	THE GREAT SCANDAL
	Ecumenism

CONCLUDING UNIT	**MISSION**
	To whom are we sent?
	As adults, how do we pass on our beliefs?
	Should we?
	Bringing up children...
	Relationships with friends...
	Skills for the challenges ahead

LEAVING OUT A UNIT, OR MATERIAL FROM A UNIT

The time needed is very difficult to quantify exactly. It is better to take longer over a unit that is proving to be very important for the group, than to be bound by having to get through all the material provided. More material has been supplied than could ever be properly covered in one session or unit. This is so as to allow for individual choice and selection. We have also tried to provide a realistic amount of background material for the non-specialist who may be a group leader. The material has been designed as a resource, to be used as comprehensively or as sparingly as is appropriate.

SCOPE FOR CELEBRATION

Moments of celebration have not been explicitly built in to the programme, since this would most probably lead to imposing an artificial and therefore unhelpful situation on the group.

As the group works and grows together, they will find that they have common values and aspirations which they will want to celebrate together. The group leaders should be alert to this, and provide whatever may be necessary in terms of time and locale to facilitate these natural celebrations. For example, you can expect celebration to be a natural part of the yearly conference.

EVALUATING THE PROGRAMME'S PROGRESS
The nature of the programme means that evaluation is automatically built into it:

> - the students are repeatedly invited to reflect on 'where they are now'; in most instances, they have to choose how they will approach each unit in the light of evaluating themselves and their attitude towards it;
> - this pattern of reflecting on a topic in the light of their experience, knowledge, and their growing understanding is repeated for each new unit;
> - the concluding unit offers the students a more thorough opportunity to evaluate their journey throughout the whole programme.

All of this happens principally at the level of opting for the group work 'approaches' and in the discussion and activity that takes place within those groups. However, there ought also to be the various worksheets and other materials, which we recommend are stored in a file/folder. These will form a necessary record of their responses; if you like, they may mark milestones on their faith journey. The students will need these to help them reflect on their own progress through the programme. It may be necessary for the programme leader to store the students' files to save them from being mislaid. Obviously, you need to be able to reassure the students that their files are being treated with proper confidentiality.

The whole notion of evaluation is one of the principal reasons for the yearly conference. As the students plan and prepare for this, they must continually try to assess the varying needs of the group as a whole, and what will be the most effective way of providing for these. It is very helpful if each conference participant fills in an evaluation sheet before leaving the conference.

THE YEARLY CONFERENCES
Our experience shows it is extremely useful to have yearly area conferences.

Young adults in the Church often feel isolated, and very much part of a minority group within their parish. The idea behind the area conference is to provide a day-long opportunity for all the young people to come together in groups from parishes, deaneries, schools, diocese, groups of schools or colleges. They gather together as 'Church' to share and celebrate their faith.

The conference should be organized and planned by the students and the teachers/group leaders together. The theme for the day should be chosen through consultation with all the various groups of people following the programme. As many students as possible should carry responsibility for the day. The input could be provided by outside speakers, the students themselves, or a combination of both. What is important is that the students feel that this is their conference.

Wherever possible, the conference should be 'off-site'.

RESOURCES

The *Search for Meaning* programme provides:

- teaching notes for group leaders. These notes are for guidance only, and should not be followed slavishly. Not every point needs to be covered.

- discussion/activity sheets for the students. They have been designed to be appropriate regardless of the group organization you choose. Again, be selective in presenting this material to the students. The early units allow for more written work in developing responses, but as the group grows in confidence and trust of one another, you will probably find you can move directly to vocal discussion. However, be sensitive to natural shyness: not everyone will feel at ease in having to speak, especially when the topics cover personal issues.

- sample posters to help students choose between the 'critical faith acceptance' and 'critical faith questioning' paths.

Remember that each unit contains:

- leader's notes which are recommendations on how to approach the presentation of each session;
- discussion/activity sheets which are the practical implementation of each session.

18

Whoever is responsible for the introductory input should also know what the students' worksheets contain, and should make whatever choices or adaptations are necessary.

OVERVIEW OF THE PROGRAMME AT WORK

This introduction has explained each of the various elements that go to make up the *Search for Meaning* programme. It may help to see, albeit in summary form, an overview of the programme as it unfolds. The chart overleaf (pages 20-21) shows this, with the main implications for the group leaders and students. The pattern displayed there repeats itself throughout all the Units, except the Concluding Unit.

Remember that Units 1 to 8 are numbered simply for ease of reference: apart from the Introductory Unit (which must come first) and the Concluding Unit (which must come last), the other Units can be used in *any* order.

FUTURE DEVELOPMENT

Because the Units are self-contained, it will be easy to develop and expand the *Search for Meaning* programme by adding new units. This is a task not just for the author and publishers, but for anyone working on faith exploration with 16-plus year-olds. Once you are familiar with the existing programme, you may find there is a topic or theme of special interest to you which might - or even should - be covered by a Unit. We do encourage you to share your suggestions with us, whether as outline ideas, or as a more developed draft of a complete unit.

We offer this book in the spirit of dialogue: we are sharing with you ideas that have helped us as we strive to make sense of our lives and purpose. We look forward to your reply, as together we *Search for Meaning*.

THE PROGRAMME	THE LEADERS	THE STUDENTS
	Establish the timetable for the programme. Establish the team of teachers/group leaders. Have a 'staff' meeting to talk through the introductory unit. Group leaders to opt for 'critical faith acceptance' or 'critical faith questioning' stance.	
INTRODUCTORY UNIT **Session 1**		Advise students that there will be a first session involving them all, at the end of which they will be invited to opt for smaller working groups, based on the two posters.
	Put up the posters so that students can sign on for small groups.	All students together in large group for input session. Students sign up for small group as they feel appropriate. Work through discussion and activities in small groups.
	Group leaders work through discussion and activities with small groups.	
Session 2	Group leaders work through discussion and activities with small groups. Pin up the list of debate topics for Session 6.	All students together in large group for input session; into small groups for discussion and activities.

Session 3	Group leaders work through discussion and activities with small groups. Work with students, as requested by them, in preparation for debate; students may invite group leader to be member of panel of speakers.	All students together in large group for input session; into small groups for discussion and activities. Vote for topic that will be debated in Session 6, so that groups can begin preparatory work and choose their panel of speakers.
Session 4	Group leaders work through discussion and activities with small groups.	All students together in large group for input session; into small groups for discussion and activities.
Session 5	Group leaders work through discussion and activities with small groups. 'Staff' meeting to talk through next unit; group leaders opt for stance.	All students together in large group for input session; into small groups for discussion and activities.
Session 6	The debate.	The debate.
THEMATIC UNIT 1 **Session 1**	Put up the posters so students can sign on for small groups. *And so on, as in Introductory Unit.*	*And so on, as in Introductory Unit.*

INTRODUCTORY UNIT
SESSION 1

This Introductory Unit is designed to help the students understand the influences which have formed their personalities and
outlook, and which have brought them to their present position
of belief.

By focusing on two individual lives the aim is to lead the
students to examine the factors that form the basis of how they
think about themselves, their relationships, and the world in
which they live.

The fact that people have been initiated into a faith community, as, for example, through baptism or some other rite,
does not guarantee they will behave in a certain fashion, nor
does it mean that they will naturally adopt the beliefs of that
community.

This can be illustrated by setting up a comparison between
two very different people, yet who belonged to the same faith
group.

Show the extracts from, on the one hand:
   * *Brother Sun, Sister Moon* (particularly of Francis leaving
   home; and of Francis before the Pope);
   * *A Man for All Seasons*;
   * material about Mother Teresa of Calcutta.
And on the other hand:
   * newsreel compilations of the build-up to World War II
   in Germany, especially the anti-Jewish actions.
(If you cannot get these videos, perhaps you could have the
students act out the scenes from the plays; or choose suitable
passages from appropriate literature.)
Draw the students' attention to the fact that:
   - both Francis/Thomas More/Mother Teresa and Hitler
   were baptized Roman Catholics;
   - both were passionately committed to, and worked
   single-mindedly for what they believed in.

Lead the discussion to consider:
- how each of these characters came to the decisions about:
    who they were;
    their future roles in life;
    their visions of the future;
- who were the main influences on each of these people;
- what circumstances effected change in their lives.

You may prefer to choose similar material from other faiths. For example:
* extracts from *Gandhi* (particularly where he is torn between those who want violence and those who don't, and he fasts);
* newsreel material about Ayatollah Khomeini, or Palestinian leaders.

DISCUSSION TOPICS
Introductory Unit   Session 1

Why do you think that Saint Francis found it necessary to leave his wealthy family? How do you think his family felt?

St.F.   A.H.

The Church in the time of Saint Francis appears to have been a very wealthy institution.
Two very different ways of living out a commitment to the Gospel are represented by the meeting in Rome between Francis and the Pope.
What is your reaction to this scene?

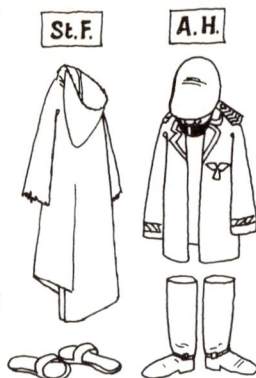

If you had to choose, where would you feel most at home:
- with Francis and his followers?
- with the established Church?

What are your reactions to the building up of Hitler's Germany in the time before World War II?
What, in your opinion, motivated Hitler to behave in the way he did?

Religion, it is claimed, was very important in the times of both Hitler and Saint Francis. How was it possible for Hitler to succeed in what he did?

Saint Francis was not popular with the established Church in his time. Many times people tried to force him to stop.
Why do you think they were not successful?

INTRODUCTORY UNIT
SESSION 2

The input for this second session is that someone speaks to the students, telling them how he/she arrived at his/her present understanding of him/herself in relation to past influences; to be willing to talk about the major landmarks in his/her life; to be open and honest about the positive, and the negative.

This speaker could be someone invited from the local community, or it could be the group leader.

Using a flipchart or blackboard, encourage the large group to share common experiences that they may have had. Encourage them to say how many of these events have really affected them personally.

The only thing that people really have in common is their humanity; everything else is unique.

Each person is at a different stage on their journey through life. For some, the route seems clear and smooth; for others it might be quite the opposite.

Illustrate that, all through life, we are discovering who we are, we are seeking and searching after truth. No one has all the answers.

The same big question seems to hang over us all:
Why am I here and what is it all for?

We need to dream; to go away and allow ourselves to be true to who we are. Then, with that knowledge, to aim high for what we feel will bring true peace and happiness.

DISCUSSION TOPICS
Introductory Unit   Session 2a

Write down the five 'best' moments in your life so far. These could be the happiest moments, moments of success, when you achieved something really difficult, or for the first time.

Write down the five 'worst' moments in your life so far. These could be the five unhappiest, or most difficult occasions.

Now number these occasions in order from one to ten according to those which have had the most effect on you and your life.

Can you say why this was? How did your life change?

If you feel able, discuss some or all of your answers with a partner, or with a small group.

DISCUSSION TOPICS
Introductory Unit   Session 2b

By this stage in your life, you have probably been through many influences and pressures, all trying to tell you the best way forward. We each need to listen to all that advice, but more importantly we each need to weigh it up and decide how we will react.
Here are four sources that have been offering you advice: what has each been telling you about which is the best way forward?

 **Parents**

Teachers

 **Friends**

Chaplain

How far have you followed this advice? Discuss this in your groups.

What are your dreams for the next two years?
What do you personally hope for?

Imagine that these dreams come true:
what do you hope to do then?

Discuss in your groups what you have put in the 'hopes and dreams' boxes.

INTRODUCTORY UNIT
SESSION 3

Having looked at two very different lifestyles in the first session, and explored some of the influences that have affected us in our own lives in the second session, the focus of this third session is to ask how we see ourselves developing.

Is it possible to do this alone?

Explore the different community settings the members of the group may have been through (it may help to write these up on the flipchart/blackboard): Family; Friends; Schooling; Clubs; Church; Employment; (Others...).

Having clarified the structures that surround us all, there are two central questions that we must face:

1. How far have these communities been positive or negative experiences for us?

Do these communities exist only for our benefit?

2. How do we see our past moulding our present, in order in turn to lead us on to future development?

What can we give to these communities?

We need to see the wholeness of who we are. The individual person is not just the sum of his/her attributes:

e.g. I'm not just someone with red hair; someone who is good at sport; etc.

Each of us is a whole person, who functions in a particular way because of a combination of many different factors.

How can each of us express our individuality, our uniqueness? Dare we? Try and construct a list of possible means:

e.g. through education, career, leisure, dress, ideals, politics, community service, etc.

Lead the session so that you have time to conclude on this key question:

Has your experience of Church helped you unfold the mystery of who you are, or does it just get in the way?

ROLE PLAY

Character 1: *You are very good looking.*
You have a boy/girl friend.

Character 2: *You are the boy/girl friend of Character 1.*

Character 3: *You are Character 1's friend.*
You know that Character 2 is going out with
Character 1 only because Character 1 is so good-looking,
and so it is good for Character 2's image.

Problem: *Character 1 thinks that he/she is in*
love with Character 2;

Character 1 tells this in
confidence to Character 3.

What happens?

POINTS FOR DISCUSSION

*   *It is one thing to see our own worth and value when we have a lot*
    going for us.
    But how do we feel if our gifts are not ones that other people rate very
    highly?

*   *Do you ever find it difficult to be the person you are?*
    Do you ever feel pressurized into being 'someone else',
    into doing things the way everyone else wants because that is more
    acceptable?

*   *Divide into pairs.*
    Without letting your partner see, write down three 'gifts' that you
    think your partner has;
    then write down three 'gifts' that you think you have.
    Compare your results, and discuss, first with your partner, then with
    the group.

*   *Do you feel that you are able to be involved in your church community*
    and accepted as the person you are?

INTRODUCTORY UNIT
SESSION 4

Having looked at 'where we are', the influences in our lives, and the need for the support of some kind of community/relationship, we now turn to explore different forms of knowledge and their relationship to faith.

How has the knowledge the students call their own, gained through their various experiences, affected their faith stance?

With the students, construct a list of different kinds of knowledge:

e.g. understanding, empathy, scientific knowledge, literary appreciation, art, etc.

Explore together the following questions:

To what extent can/should faith be based on knowledge?

To what extent can knowledge destroy faith?

Are faith and knowledge compatible/complementary?

Is it possible to have complete knowledge?

If we had complete knowledge, would we need faith?

Show how and in what ways each of these questions relates to Christian faith.

End the input by playing *I know that my Redeemer liveth* from Handel's *Messiah*. Ask the question:

In what ways could this be said to be knowledge?

DISCUSSION TOPICS
Introductory Unit   Session 4

Try to recall your earliest memories of being told about God.
Write them down here:

Think back to times when you might have felt that you did believe
there was such a person as God or Jesus.
Has this continued? Has it changed? Has it ceased?
Try and offer reasons for this:

What do you think about the contribution of scientific knowledge to our
understanding of the existence of God?
For example, does science help our understanding of God?
Or does science explain away God's existence?
Write down how you feel about this,
and then discuss it in your
group.

$x \cdot y^2$ 739
$= 42^4$ $7°c \times 9$
$* -\frac{1}{2} \times 6^{42}$

LIVERPOOL HOPE UNIVERSITY COLLEGE

INTRODUCTORY UNIT
SESSION 5

Some people believe that life on earth is all that there is. What might be the source of motivation for such people?

Think back to Session 1: how were Francis and Hitler driven or motivated by what they perceived to be the purpose of life? How did this influence their behaviour?

Explore these questions:
Is there an after-life?
Is life about 'getting to Heaven'?
What about Hell . . .?
What are Heaven and Hell? Are they places?

You may find the following useful to illustrate ideas about Heaven and Hell:
-From literature, a potential illustration would be Charles Dickens' *A Christmas Carol*: compare the two characters Bob Cratchit and Scrooge and their respective motivation; use extracts from Milton's *Paradise Lost* and *Paradise Regained*.
- Show prints of doorway relief, Bourges Cathedral.
- Use extracts from Augustine's *City of God* and Ignatius' *Spiritual Exercises*.
- For biblical images, see Revelation 19:11 - 22:5, or John 14:1-4.
- There are many passages in the Koran about Heaven and Hell which could be appropriate, and interesting to compare with the Christian scriptures.

*   *Imagine that you
    are baby sitting
    at home.
    Your four-year-old
    sister suddenly asks
    you:
    what happens when
    we die?*

    *What would you
    answer?*

*   **And if the same four-year-old then asks:**
    how do we get to Heaven?
    what happens if we don't go to Heaven?
    What would you answer?

    Divide into pairs to work out your replies.
    Then discuss the following in your group:

*   **Would you give an answer to a child
    that you did not believe yourself?**

*   **Do your own personal views on either/both of the original
    questions differ from what you would tell your
    four-year-old sister?**

*   **Would you say that you lead a 'good' life?
    e.g. being kind and thoughtful to others?**

*   **Why do you do this?**

From SEARCH FOR MEANING, published by Geoffrey Chapman, © Judith Russi SSMN 1990.
Multiple copies may be made only by the institution which has purchased a master set.

'If God did not exist,
it would be necessary
to invent him.'
(Voltaire)

'God is a substitute
for lack of knowledge.'

'It is only a matter of time
before science answers
all the mysteries of life.'

'Heaven and Hell
are only images,
conjured up to control
the superstitious masses.'

UNIT 1
SESSION 1
MORALITY IN A PLURALISTIC SOCIETY

Down through the ages there has never been one moral code for all human beings. Different cultures, in different parts of the world, adhere to very strict, but different, moral codes.

Explore how moral decision making began.

The Old Testament offers one (very influential) moral code, but long before the Bible there were well established societies with their own rules, laws and moral codes.

Perhaps the real tension in moral decision making for our society today lies not so much in trying to be faithful to one particular moral code, but rather in having to cope with several moral codes within one society.

> e.g. Cannibals are a highly moral people: they adhere to a very strict moral code. They eat human flesh - but never the flesh of one of their own tribe.
>
> Christians are a highly moral people; they do not eat human flesh, and consider it immoral to do so.

How do we decide which of these groups is acting in a moral, or immoral, fashion?

Is it ever possible to make such a judgement?

It is one thing to decide on a moral code for ourselves, but quite another to impose it on others. Not everyone looks at life in the same way. There are very different philosophies of life, which in turn imply very different attitudes towards life and towards relationships with other people.

You may find Chapter 1 of *Christian Morality and You* by J. Finlay and M. Pennock (Ave Maria Press, 1976) useful for this session.

35

* In small groups,
make a list of topics, beliefs or values which concern moral issues
and about which you know there is the most varied response.

Why do you think there is such difference in opinion on these
issues?   Is it because people are unclear about them?

* Would you personally be happier to have someone to tell you
the difference between right and wrong?
or do you prefer to make up your own mind?

* Do you think people in this country are tolerant or intolerant
towards people who 'break the rules'?
Towards people who don't accept the norms of society?
   e.g. what is the general attitude to:
      - shoplifting, or receiving stolen goods?
      - 'borrowing' things from work or the office?
      - tax dodging?
      - dole cheating?

UNIT 1
SESSION 2
THE CHRISTIAN CODE

The Christian code of morality is based on a personal relationship between the individual Christian and God. An essential element in this relationship is that it is something far deeper than merely that of the fidelity of a disciple to a great moral teacher; deeper even than the fidelity proper to a deep human relationship.

Even within the Christian code there are, and have been throughout history, significant variations of interpretation as to what may be right or wrong (for example, the difference between Christian churches on divorce and remarriage, etc.).

THE OLD TESTAMENT LAW

Great emphasis was laid on keeping numerous laws, rules and regulations, so as to live a 'righteous' life, and achieve salvation.

The Ten Commandments can only be properly understood within the overall context of the Covenant between God and his people.

Today, the 'new people' of God also live in obedience to the Ten Commandments as a willing response to God's loving call to them to be his people.

The first three of the Ten Commandments emphasize our need to 'love God above all else'; the other seven to 'love neighbour as self'.

THE NEW TESTAMENT LAW

This is expressed in the Beatitudes, the great Law of Love. This has to be seen in the context of Jesus' assertion that he comes to fulfil the Law, not to abolish or change it. He gives the Law its full meaning; his emphasis is not on external observance, but on the heart.

He emphasizes love, forgiveness. Cf. Gospel examples of:
- the Good Samaritan;
- the lost sheep;

- the woman at the well;
- Mary Magdalene;
- 'Whatsoever you do to the least of these, you do to me'.

CHANGES

In the 1960s, women always covered their heads in church. It was considered 'wrong' not to.

Only a generation ago, Catholics were not permitted to attend services in any other Christian church without the permission of their parish priest.

In the 1960s, children who had to attend non-Catholic schools were not allowed to attend morning assembly with the other children.

What is it that has changed?
- the law?
- our understanding?
- the Church?
- our attitudes?
- the way we interpret the law?

In a multi-faith group, Muslim students may be able to find differences of tradition between different families, or between Muslims from different backgrounds; lead the students to distinguish, too, between tradition and the actual teaching of the Koran.

DISCUSSION TOPICS
Unit 1 Session 2

For each of the following quotations, say whether you agree, or disagree, and give your reasons:

> Love is the most important factor in moral decision making.

> I don't go to church any more because those who do go are only there for show or to keep the letter of the law.

> The Christian moral code was fine for 2,000 years ago, but in this modern day it's become unrealistic.

In the *Gospels* there are many examples of Jesus mixing with people who were known to be great sinners.
The *Gospels* show that Jesus was very popular with these outcasts.

*   Why do you think this was?

The Christian tradition has always taught that Sunday should be a day of rest and for giving time to God, e.g. by going to church, by prayer, by spiritual reading, etc.

*   What do you think of the way Sunday is observed in our society?

*   In what ways do you think it should be different, and why?

UNIT 1
SESSION 3
TENSION BETWEEN CODES

This session will explore the tensions that inevitably arise between
  - religious (and particularly Christian) moral code;
  - cultural code;
  - civil code.

A first necessary stage is to clarify what each of these codes is. With the students, establish a working definition for each of them.

The next step is to explore the inter-relationship between these codes.

For example, changes in the cultural code of morality (i.e. what society perceives as acceptable/unacceptable) can bring pressure to bear which results in a change in the civil code.

- an 'old' law can become obsolete in new cultural circumstances, and so the law is repealed, or changed (e.g. the law no longer demands that those guilty of theft be hanged or deported to a penal colony!);

- equally, new cultural circumstances, i.e. changes in society's habits, can demand new laws (e.g. to deal with drunken driving; to deal with drugs; to deal with football hooliganism; etc.).

With the students, develop an understanding of these relationships through specific examples:
  - birth control (where religious and cultural codes clash);
  - abortion (where there is opposition between the religious and the civil codes);
  - hanging (cultural and religious pressure bringing about a change in the civil law);
  - experiments on embryos (development of cultural attitudes which will influence law-making);

- right to vote (extended to women because of cultural pressure; similar pressure now extends the voting age to 18);
- environmental issues (cultural pressure building up will lead to new laws, e.g. on exhaust gas emissions, etc.).

How can an individual decide what or who is 'right'?

Three crucial points to bear in mind in trying to understand this:

1. Each person or idea with which I come into contact is only a *potential* source of morality; nothing can become an *actual* source of morality for me, until I choose to make it so. In other words, *until I believe that it is right for me.*

2. There are forces in the world which are harmful, which are sinful and evil. But we cannot depend on an institution or an authoritative body to alert us to these, or in making the decision for us as to what is evil. It is in the very nature of the heavy machinery of institutions to react slowly, and in today's fast-changing world, institutions (the Church included) are not always able to keep up.

3. It is all very well to understand morality as being true to what I believe; but are we always sure what we really believe?

You may find this quote from Gandhi pertinent:
'If you Christians were more like your Christ, the whole world would be Christian.'

DISCUSSION TOPICS
Unit 1   Session 3

Can you give one example of civil law that you would say is immoral?
Why do you consider it immoral?

Is there anything about your life at the moment (e.g. as a sixth former,
or as a member of some club, or because of your family) which you
feel obliged to tolerate or comply with, even though you don't think it
is right? What is it, and what are your reasons?

If you belong to a Church, is there any part of that church's moral
teaching that you don't agree with?
What is it, and why don't you agree?

Of the three moral codes above (civil; cultural; religious) which has the
most influence on your life and the way you behave? And why?

UNIT 1
SESSION 4
MORAL CODES AND INDIVIDUAL CHOICE

The individual's ability to choose is a fundamental trait. This is an accepted fact, established by the social sciences (i.e. it is not just a theological premise).

Human beings are not bound, as are animals, by their instincts.

They can choose to change; to improve their lot; they can to a large extent direct their future. This is what is meant by the traditional expression that human beings possess *free will*.

Work this out with the students by means of examples - which can be fictitious ones: e.g.

> you may belong to a bigoted family that believes that everyone who lives north of Watford is lazy; and that if they're out of work, it's because they prefer to do nothing and sponge off the dole. As you get older you come into contact with people from the North, and discover how they are powerless to do much against the blight of unemployment. At this stage, you are free to remain with your former ignorant opinion, or you can choose to change.

'LOVE'

One of the greatest proofs of our freedom is that we can willingly desire the good of another person, or we can will them harm.

Love is choosing 'for' others, wanting them to 'grow' and 'develop'.

'UNIQUE'

In the introductory unit we established the notion of each person's uniqueness. The context there was of understanding myself as unique, but equally we need to acknowledge that each person is a unique being.

And yet this very uniqueness depends on others, because we are also *social* beings. How we treat other people depends very much on how we see them in relation to ourselves and what we believe.

VARYING OPINIONS

Use concrete examples to work out with the students how opinions can vary:

> e.g. You come across some friends, gathered outside the Sixth Form block, smoking. They offer to share with you a cigarette which they say will 'set you free'. Realizing that you are being offered 'pot', what would your reaction be?
> - 'It's wrong';
> - 'It's illegal';
> - 'It's harmless';
> - 'OK. Lots of people do it';
> - 'Smoking is against school rules'.

> e.g. You know that two members of the Youth Club are selling stolen goods to younger people. What would your reaction be?
> - would you say something to them?
> - say nothing?
> - receive goods from them at a 'good' price?
> - tell someone in authority? If so, who? And how?

Once you have worked through the particularities of the examples, focus on this:

> - is there one right answer? On what grounds did you judge your answer to be 'right' or 'wrong'?

SIN

One definition of sin characterizes it as the transgression of God's known will, or of any principle or law regarded as embodying this divine will. Sin was further categorized in degrees, under the broad headings of mortal sin, venial sin, and original sin.

Today, the emphasis is not so much concerned with establishing which actions might be properly described as 'sinful', but rather in terms of the question: how are we responding to the love which God has for us personally and for all other people on earth?

So a better definition of sin would be that it is a rejection of God's love; a refusal of an opportunity to accept his love and pass it on to others.

Sin is a sign of inhumanity and immaturity; it is something that destroys our personality, inhibits our true development, and leads to ultimate frustration.

DISCUSSION TOPICS
Unit 1 Session 4a

Imagine that you are the parent of a pre-school child.
List the important values that you would like them to have.

Compare your answers with a friend. How do they differ?

Discuss your values with the rest of the group.
Are there areas common to everyone in the group?
If so, put a tick in the box alongside the relevant value.

If your child did not do as you asked or expected, how would you correct him/her?

Think back to your own childhood: what made you 'be good'? What was most effective in teaching you to follow a moral code?

DISCUSSION TOPICS
Unit 1 Session 4b

**As your child becomes a teenager,
how would you cope with their moral training?**

**Would it be the same for a boy as for a girl?
If different, in what ways would it be different?**

**How 'strict' do you think parents should be?
Give examples.**

**Have you ever experienced religion being used as a threat to make
you do something?
e.g. 'You'll go to Hell unless . . .'**

UNIT 1
SESSION 5
THE CONSEQUENCES OF
MORAL CHOICES

The commonest consequence for individuals who know they have made a wrong moral decision is guilt. Worries about personal failings beset some people all the time, and all of us at some time.

Christians believe that God will forgive any sin again and again, as long as the individual is truly sorry. Some Christian churches have formalized the expression of God's forgiveness in a special rite. Roman Catholics, for example, celebrate the sacrament of reconciliation.

God never punishes us for our sins - rather, we do that ourselves; or perhaps others punish us because of what we choose to do. God treats us as adults who are no longer in need of constant parental interventions.

Have the students discuss the following statements. Ask them first of all what they feel might be the consequences of each:

> 'A woman should be allowed to obtain an abortion whenever she wishes; it's nobody else's business.'

> 'People shouldn't be pressurized into getting married; they should be left free to move from one partner to another if they want to.'

> 'Old people and the chronically sick should be allowed to ask that their life be ended if they so wish.'

'If sixth formers are put in charge of younger pupils, they should be allowed to punish them if necessary.'

'Children who feel they aren't being fairly treated by their parents should be allowed to leave them, and be supported by the state.'

Then encourage the students to examine each statement again from the following standpoints:
- someone who is very religious;
- someone who is nominally religious;
- someone who is not religious at all.

Discuss this question with the group:
- is it true, do you think, that someone who is not religious or who does not believe in God, cannot be a moral person?

DISCUSSION TOPICS
Unit 1 Session 5

Decision making about important matters in life is never easy. Making the right decision is difficult enough, but making the wrong one can leave the individual not only in a mess, but also feeling frustrated and guilty.

With a partner, share an experience when you had an important decision to make, and it turned out to be the wrong one.

Discuss what you think of this statement:

> *The only real mistake that people can make is one they don't learn from.*

Here are three scenarios:

- *a 15-year-old girl runs away from home; she hitches a lift in a lorry going to London.*

- *a 16-year-old pupil gets angry and punches a teacher.*

- *a fifth former, under pressure due to exams, begins stealing secretly from his parents' cocktail cabinet.*

EITHER: *discuss these scenarios and their possible consequences*

OR: *divide into groups and act out one of the scenes.*

Make sure that you show
- *what led to the situation*
- *how it could turn out*
- *how it might be resolved*

From SEARCH FOR MEANING, published by Geoffrey Chapman, © Judith Russi SSMN 1990.
Multiple copies may be made only by the institution which has purchased a master set.

'No one has the right to decide
what is right or wrong
for another person.'

'Being a Christian
is no more morally demanding
than being anything else.'

'Where there is no freedom,
there is no responsibility;
where there is no responsibility,
there is no morality.'

UNIT 2
SESSION 1
CALLED TO BE . . .?

IMAGE OF SELF

Seeing ourselves as others see us is not at all easy. Much of what we think we are is very tied up with what we would like to be. One way to discover what others think of us is to be open to their description of us. The photocopiable hand-out offers a simple exercise in exchanging descriptions with a partner or a friend.

Sixteen-plus year-olds already have a fair amount of experience of what life is about. They will each have, not only that experience, but hopes, ambitions and dreams, as well as fears or dreads.

Encourage the students to look, as honestly as they are able, at where they are now as compared to where they would like to be. Push them to be sure that whatever decision they propose is what they really want. Encourage them to formulate their reasons, i.e. how did they come to make that decision?

Sooner or later we all have to face the nagging question of 'what I really want from life'. Have the students face this, individually first, and then in group discussion. It may help to divide the topic into 'areas' of life, e.g.

what do I want for myself?

what do I want in terms of relationships?

what are my ambitions?

INDIVIDUAL PRIORITIES

Help the students to discern trends, i.e. that different groups in society will have different priorities:

- e.g. 'yuppies': what is important to this group?

Have the students identify various groupings in society, and compare them, and what their priorities are:

- what is each group actually looking for?

- what forces can you detect which dictate their choice of priorities?

We live in a very mixed society. The individual worth of each person will be very different depending on how they are being assessed. Individuals can be 'valued' for a range of reasons:

- because they are good at their job;
- because they are intelligent;
- because they are wealthy;
- because they are attractive, good-looking;
- because of their personality;
- etc.

DISCUSSION TOPICS
Unit 2 Session 1a

**Work out a description of the person you think you are.
Begin by listing your main qualities, key faults:**

Exchange your description with a partner or a friend, and see if you can recognize one another!

Write down briefly what you hope for from life:

for yourself	relationships	ambitions

Share these with the group. Are there any common hopes?

As a group, work out the five qualities you think are the most important in a person.	

DISCUSSION TOPICS
Unit 2 Session 1b

ROLE PLAY

Scenario 1:   *Main character is a boy, aged 16.*
He is quite bright, and should get three A levels.
He wants to be a male nurse.
His parents disagree, and say he should be a doctor.
The parents visit the school to speak to the head of the
sixth form, to try to have pressure brought on the boy
to 'see sense'.

What happens?

Scenario 2:   *Main character is either a boy or a girl,*
going for a job interview.
The potential
employer says not
sure if the job can
be offered to the
young person
because their
school references
say they were
always 'a source
of distraction'.

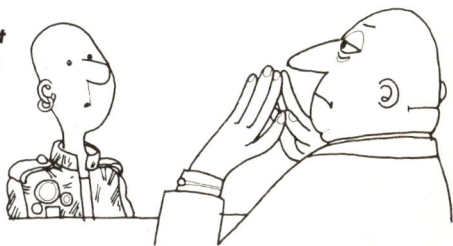

What happens?

Scenario 3:   *Main character is a girl, aged 17.*
She is going out with a boy aged 22.
They want to get engaged.
The boy has a job, but the girl is still at school.
The girl's parents say the boy is 'not good enough'.

What happens?

From SEARCH FOR MEANING, published by Geoffrey Chapman, © Judith Russi SSMN 1990.
Multiple copies may be made only by the institution which has purchased a master set.

UNIT 2
SESSION 2
CALLED TO BE WITH OTHERS

Human beings, despite their uniqueness, are essentially social beings. We need to be with other people; my life can only take on shape and meaning in relationship to others.

What kind of relationship towards others might I choose as my lifestyle?
- to remain a single person;
- to marry;
- to live in community with like-minded people;
- to become a member of a religious community;
- to become a priest;
- to live with a friend.

Again, the key discussion should focus on deciding what are the real priorities in my life:
- to marry and have a family?
- to marry, but to have a successful job that does not allow time for 'family'?
- to remain single because of the need to be free for my work?
- to remain single because of a religious calling?
- to marry, raise a family, and hold a meaningful job that will support the family in comfort?

SOCIAL PRESSURES
Again, the individual does not make such choices in isolation, but is subject to various pressures. In today's world is there perhaps an 'anti-commitment' pressure? Many people prefer not to commit themselves to anything that is binding; they want to be free to move in and out of relationships as they please. Do we live in an age of 'individualism'?

Remember to ensure the discussion includes consideration of the implications:
- a life with no ties?
- a life that has commitment to a person/to people?

UNIQUENESS
Within all this talk of relationship, we need to remember that no two people are alike. The contribution that one can make cannot be made by another.

In other words each of us has an individual vocation; I am called to be . . .

Each person has to discover what his/her 'vocation' is: e.g.
- what will bring me true happiness?
- where can I find true fulfilment?
- where or in what way can my gifts best be used to help others?

DISCUSSION TOPICS
Unit 2 Session 2

What do you think of these statements?
Do you agree, or disagree? Give your reasons:

> Most people get married because that's what's expected of them.

> We live in an age of individualism and anti-commitment.

When you leave school, do you hope:
- *to live at home?*
- *to live with a friend?*
- *to live on your own?*

Do you feel that you have a 'special calling'?
        that you have something to bring to the world
        which no one else can?

ROLE PLAY

Scenario: **Four of you are sharing a flat.**
             Things are not going too well.
             Some people never wash
             up or help clean.
             Another keeps inviting
             friends round without
             asking anyone else first .

             What do you do about it?

UNIT 2
SESSION 3
WHAT KIND OF LIFE . . .?

This unit builds on the groundwork established by Sessions 1 and 2, focusing clearly and specifically on three lifestyles:
- the single life;
- the married life;
- the religious/ordained life.

THE SINGLE LIFE
Either:
Invite a single person to share with the students the reasons for and implications of their choice of the single life.
Or:
Use the interview with Jane*.

THE MARRIED LIFE
Either:
Invite a married couple to share with the students the reasons for and the implications of their choice of the married life.
Or:
Use the interview with James*.

THE RELIGIOUS/ORDAINED LIFE
Either:
Invite a priest or a religious brother or sister to share with the students the reasons for and the implications of their choice of their way of life.
Or:
Read the account of Sister Emmanuelle.

* The interviews could either be read out, or, if you have access to the technical facilities, perhaps two students could prepare an audio or video tape, as if it were a radio or TV interview.

THE SINGLE LIFE

Interviewer   I'd like to talk to you today about being single. The first thing I'd like to raise with you is, how do people react when they realize you have never been married?

Jane   You make it sound as though being single is something to hide. I'm not ashamed of being single!

Interviewer   I'm sorry, that wasn't my intention.

Jane   That's all right. I'm not offended. People's reaction? Well, it has changed over the years. When I was in my early thirties, there was a considerable amount of patronizing pity. Women seemed to think that because I hadn't married I was a failure. And men often thought that I was missing out on life, and so I was 'fair game', someone they could flirt with quite safely. Few seemed to understand that I had not been overlooked, but that I had made a conscious decision to stay single and celibate.

Interviewer   You imply that things are different now, though.

Jane   Yes, to some extent. Of course, there are still those who think I'm strange because I'm not married, nor a nun nor a nurse - strangely enough, it has always been acceptable to be single if you're a nurse. But there are more and more people who accept me, and others like me, for what we really are: people who are single because they chose to stay single.

Interviewer   You speak of your 'conscious decision' not to get married. Can you say a little more about how you came to make that choice?

Jane   I'll try! I lived through the swinging sixties, and at the time I thought I was enjoying myself - but it wasn't really enough. The pursuit of pleasure and material things just wasn't satisfying enough. My faith was still there, but it had become mechanical and superficial and very shaky.

Interviewer   Didn't you form any close relationships during this time?

Jane   Yes, certainly I did. In fact, I came very close to marriage, but I'm afraid I didn't feel able to make the kind of commitment that marriage demanded. I couldn't face the responsibility of a husband, children, house . . .

Interviewer   Forgive me for interrupting, but weren't these rather superficial excuses? Other people have to face these same responsibilities, and would say that if you loved the other person, all these seeming obstacles could be overcome.

Jane Well, perhaps that's true for them - I can only speak for myself. I was in love, and it wasn't an easy decision to have to make. It was heart-breaking. You know, sometimes if you love a person enough, you have to let them go. I knew I couldn't be the kind of wife he needed, so it was better we did not marry.

Interviewer Was that when you made your decision to opt for the single life?

Jane No, not then. After that episode, I worked abroad for a while. When I came back I spent a long time trying to decide which direction I wanted my life to take. I enjoyed my own company; I enjoyed my job; and I had become very involved in parish life. I came to the conclusion that my life was already full and fulfilled, and there was no room for the responsibility of husband and children.

Interviewer This was how long ago?

Jane Oh, about twenty years ago.

Interviewer In all that time have you had any regrets?

Jane Regrets? No, not really. Mind you, if I'm honest there are occasions when I feel low, and I'd like to have a shoulder to cry on. But then, I have close enough friends for that.

Interviewer We all need someone or something to belong to. Do you find you have this in the single life?

Jane Yes, indeed I do. Sometimes I feel my life's not my own! I have a circle of close friends. I'm very close to my sisters and my nieces and nephews. Now I have my elderly parents living with me, and there are a number of sick and elderly parishioners I visit.

Interviewer Would you recommend the single life to others?

Jane It's a decision others must make for themselves. But I must say that if people accepted the idea of a vocation to the single life as an alternative to marriage, there would be fewer unhappy people.

Interviewer You speak of your decision to be single and celibate. Have you found it difficult to cope with this part of your decision?

Jane When I was younger, certainly it was difficult - but I made my decision quite freely. I thought it was worth making; I felt it was also worth keeping. A marriage has to be worked for, it doesn't just happen. So too with the single life. Nothing worth having comes easily.

Interviewer   One last question. Has your faith helped you?

Jane   That's the easiest question so far! Yes, my faith helped all the way. It helped me to see that every life - married, single, widowed, or even divorced - is important and has a part to play.

Interviewer   Thank you for talking so openly and frankly with me.

THE MARRIED LIFE

Interviewer   *Addressing the 'audience'.*

Hello. Let me introduce my guest to you. His name is James, and he is twenty-six. Four years ago he was involved in a serious car accident.

Addressing the guest.

Welcome, James. Do you mind if I ask you some questions about your life over the past five years?

James   No, not at all. I've got past being upset at what's happened and I can talk about it now.

Interviewer   James, I believe you were planning to get married when you were 21. But it never happened. Why was that?

James   Yes, in fact it was just two months before I was due to get married to Carol that the accident happened. I was in a head-on smash-up with a lorry on the M1. I lost my sight and the use of my legs. To put it bluntly, Carol just could not cope with me. I used to be very bitter about her breaking off our engagement, but now I'm not. She was honest, and I'm grateful for that. I would have hated her if she'd just married me because she felt sorry for me, or was too scared to call it off. It wouldn't have lasted anyway.

Interviewer   How did this make you feel about marriage? Weren't you worried about ever being able to marry?

James   Of course I was! Wouldn't you? It was hell for the first two years. I couldn't bear anyone coming to see me. I think if I had been able to see, it wouldn't have been so bad.

Interviewer   So how did you overcome this?

James   Well, it was Pete, really. Of all my friends, he was the only one who stayed faithful. I can understand why people were embarrassed and didn't feel easy about coming to visit. But Pete was different. He walked into my room one night and said, as cool as you like, 'Right, mate. You're coming to the pub.' I won't repeat what I said to him! When you're in a wheelchair you can't really stop yourself being taken where you don't want to go.

That night was the beginning of a new life for me. After a few pints, people I used to know realized that under all the scars, I was still the same bloke. I needed friends and people just like they did.

Pete called for me three times a week. That's how I met Jackie, who's now my wife. At first she was just one of the group. I liked her because she just treated me normally - called me a clumsy twit if I spilt my beer, and that kind of thing. I knew she liked me as a person and that there was no need to be nervous about her just being nice to me because she felt sorry for me.

Interviewer So when was it that the possibility of marriage came up?

James It was funny, really. She just asked me! Jackie would come round each evening and tell me all about her day. She was also helping me to type so I could keep in touch with people, and maybe get myself a job. We had been close friends for about a year when, cool as anything, one evening she said, 'Well, James, when are we going to get married, then?'

Interviewer How did you react to that?

James All the past hurt and fears just flooded back. I was really afraid that this might be another let-down. We talked all night. I realized that Jackie was more than a friend. I loved her very much. But I was afraid that I wouldn't be much of a husband for her. We knew it wouldn't be easy. A year later we were married. Some of our relations were very unsure about what we were doing. But it's our life, and we don't pretend with one another.

Interviewer So how do you find married life now?

James We love each other very much. Every day there are problems to be sorted out. But together we can do it. I don't think I'd have survived on my own. We've got a council house that's been specially adapted. I take care of the house, and now that I can type, I do some work at home for a couple of businesses. That way I can earn quite a bit of money. Jackie goes out to work - she has a good job with Marks and Spencer.

Interviewer   What about children, James?

James   We would both love to have a family. But that will need careful thinking about. We both feel we need time to get ourselves sorted out.

THE RELIGIOUS LIFE
Sister Emmanuelle

Sister Emmanuelle Cinquin was born in 1909. She became a nun with the Sisters of Our Lady of Sion in 1929. It was a missionary order, and although she had always wanted to work among the poor, having chosen to be a nun, she obeyed the orders of her Superior, and taught in schools for the daughters of the privileged class in Turkey, Tunisia and Egypt.

However, in 1963, while teaching in a school in Alexandria, she became increasingly aware of the stark contrast between the lives of the privileged girls she was teaching, and the lives of the city's poor. She managed to persuade her Order to allow her to teach in the slum quarters. This experience reinforced her yearning to be with the poor, and the Second Vatican Council made this possible.

In 1971 she reached retirement age, but instead of taking life a little more easy, she was at last freed from her Order's normal discipline and allowed to live independently in Egypt, whilst still remaining within her Order.

Soon she settled among the ragpickers of Cairo. These people are known as the *zabbaleen,* which means 'people who collect dung'. They were despised and ignored, left to live and die on the dung-heap without anyone caring whatsoever. Some 2,500 men, women and children make their living from the rubbish they collect. It is not only their life, but their home, for their shanty town is built on the rubbish tip itself.

There is no sewerage, no running water. But there are thousands of flies, and an overpowering stench of rotting food. The *zabbaleen* sell what they can, and eat whatever scraps they can, or feed them to the pigs and chickens they try to raise.

Sister Emmanuelle lives with these *zabbaleen,* in a shack measuring about 9 feet by 5 feet. Her only luxury is an earth closet, to which she keeps the key. She felt that only by living among them and as one of them could she really gain their confidence, and so be able to help them better. By sharing their wretchedness, she could offer counsel and example. She offered them first aid, psychological as well as medical; she started a kindergarten, adult literacy classes and sewing lessons. She was able to give them small gifts of things she begged from the rich of Cairo. The heart of her work was helping people in their struggle to live. Although there was great family loyalty among the *zabbaleen*, children did not know how to be children, since they were expected to work as soon as they could walk. Not surprisingly, there was considerable crime in such a place where only the fittest survived.

Sister Emmanuelle became respected and loved by these people because she became one of them. She treated all alike, whether Christian or Muslim. She did not try to convert them to Christianity. She said, 'I am here to love and to share. I have a model in Christ. What more did he do with his life?'

She maintains that people need to be loved; to be loved for what they are, not what we would like them to be. Beautiful or ugly, rich or poor, good or bad, honest or dishonest, gentle or violent, Christian or non-Christian; they are all God's children and we love them for that.

Now that she is in her eighties, she does not spend all her time among the ragpickers, though she has not stopped working on their behalf. She spends a lot of time travelling the world, collecting money, speaking to national and international government officials and organizations such as CAFOD, OXFAM and the World Bank, all with the aim of helping her beloved *zabbaleen* and all those like them throughout the world.

Of her life and work she says, 'My attempts to help them are often doomed to failure, but if my passing among them has left them with a single reminder that "God is love", I will not have been useless to them. A divine seed will have been planted amidst the filth of the garbage, and in the midst of death, life will blossom anew.'

Do you think it is more difficult for women to remain single than it is for men? Give your reasons:

On the single life:
- *single people often argue that they experience more freedom in their relationships because they are not married.*

What do you think of such an argument?

On the married life:

How would you feel about marrying someone who was disabled or who had had a serious accident?

On the religious life:
- *religious often talk of a calling from God to give their whole life for others.*

Do you think it is necessary to be a nun or a brother in order to do this work?

What do you think a religious vocation is?

UNIT 2
SESSION 4
FOCUS ON THE FAMILY

The aim of this unit is to encourage the students to reflect realistically on the implications of opting for marriage in today's world. Try and steer a happy course between a doom and gloom pessimism, and an artificially rosy, romantic view.

The starting point, exchanging ideas on why so many marriages break down, may seem to be a negative one: but the objective is to be clear about the difficulties, so as to be better placed to deal with them (should this be their choice). In other words, to progress from considering things as 'threats' to seeing them as 'challenges'.

1. FAMILY UNDER THREAT?

The pressures of life today mean that marriage and family life are under threat:

- there is the cost of living; children are expensive!
- social attitudes are changing: no one is surprised if a woman opts for a career instead of children; women are no longer expected to stay at home and look after children.
- divorce is an accepted fact of life.
- common-law partnerships are on the increase; why marry and have to go through the bother of divorce? If it doesn't work out they can go their different ways.
- there are an increasing number of single-parent families; they do not feel as stigmatized as they once did; and social services can help.
- some people are put off marriage by fear of the future; threat of unemployment; the nuclear threat.
- some people feel unable to make a commitment.
- some people feel marriage would destroy their career prospects.
- for some, their existing family ties stand in the way of marriage.

2. 'TO LOVE AND TO CHERISH'

Despite all these potential difficulties and obstacles, marriage and family life is still the lifestyle that most people opt for. Why is this?

> - because it helps answer a deep felt need to be loved and to give love.
> - because it helps answer a deep felt need for security and the desire to belong.
> - because of the deep felt need to find happiness and fulfilment in children.

Encourage the students to explore these basic needs that marriage seems to answer.

Some of the discussion questions are designed to lead from this discovery of the positive side of marriage to ways in which the 'positive' can be encouraged, or at least protected from threat.

3. WHOM GOD HAS JOINED . . .

The Christian religion, like other religions, puts a high value on marriage and family life.

Encourage the students to discuss why this is so.

Explore, as appropriate, that it has religious value and significance precisely because it is so deeply human.

Christians believe that marriage is a sacrament: that through their love for each other, the partners come to know something of God's love.

DISCUSSION TOPICS
Unit 2   Session 4

 **Why do you think so many marriages break up?**

Share your thoughts with the group.

Make a list of the things that you think are essential for a happy marriage:

Share your thoughts with the group, and discuss.

What could be done to improve the quality of your family life together?

Share your thoughts with <u>one</u> other person in the group.

With one other person from your group imagine that you have your own family. Work out how you would like to see your family life together:
    e.g. will you have meals together?
    will the children be expected to help?

Draw up a family charter together on a large sheet of paper, and then justify your decisions to the rest of the group.

From SEARCH FOR MEANING, published by Geoffrey Chapman, © Judith Russi SSMN 1990.
Multiple copies may be made only by the institution which has purchased a master set.

UNIT 2
SESSION 5
PEOPLE OF GOD?

The aim of this unit is to explore the wider, and truer, meaning of 'vocation'. Christians believe that God calls each one of us to continue the task of redeeming the world, little by little, in whatever way we can, spreading the kingdom of heaven on earth.

But there are two aspects to this 'calling' or 'vocation', which are inter-related:

on the one hand each person has an individual vocation;

on the other hand there is a responsibility to the vocation of the Christian community, i.e. the Church.

Together, as a community, we are called

- to live the Gospel.
- to witness to the standards of Jesus Christ.
- to give first place to those who are rejected by society.
- to take sides with the poor and disadvantaged.
- to work continually for a better world, a more just society.

The word 'Christians' was first applied to the followers of Jesus by non-believers. The Christians' sense of community was proverbial: 'see how these Christians love each other'.

In our own time Fidel Castro said of the Little Brothers of Charles de Foucauld, 'if the Christian Church lived as these men do, all Cuba would be Christian'.

The implication of baptism is that we are called to live in community with all who are baptized, caring for each other.

In many places, especially Latin America and the Philippines, Christians have been rediscovering their sense of Church through developing 'basic Christian communities'. Quite simply, these are groups of local people who come together each evening to share the Gospel, to see to the needs of each person (principally by sharing what little everyone has), and together to find ways of building their lifestyle on the Gospel and its values.

Accepting the challenge of being a Christian is to commit oneself to a radical lifestyle; a way of life whose roots are in the Gospel. Put simply, this means a life where everyone else has to come first.

DISCUSSION TOPICS
Unit 2 Session 5

Make a list of what you think are the distinctive characteristics of a Christian:

JOB CENTRE

MESSIAH
WANTED
MUST HAVE
COMMUNICATIONS
SKILLS

YES/NO	
YES/NO	
YES/NO	
YES/NO	
YES/NO	
YES/NO	
YES/NO	
YES/NO	
YES/NO	

Compare your list with those compiled by others in your group.

Do you think the church or community you belong to, or know of, displays these characteristics?
(Mark the characteristics YES or NO, as appropriate)
Discuss your answers.

In the early Church, according to the Acts of the Apostles, Christians lived in community. People shared all that they owned and took care of one another.
Is this possible in today's world?
Would you like to live in that kind of society today?
Give your reasons for your answers.

Do you have any sense of responsibility for looking after people who are not necessarily related to you?
How far do you think you should go in this respect?

From SEARCH FOR MEANING, published by Geoffrey Chapman, © Judith Russi SSMN 1990.
Multiple copies may be made only by the institution which has purchased a master set.

'Marriage
is an outdated system,
and should be abolished.'

'Marriage and the family
are institutions
which have stood
the test of time
and should be protected
at all costs.'

'Vocation
is a religious notion
which has little relevance
in the real world.'

UNIT 3
SESSION 1
WHAT DO WE MEAN BY COMMUNITY?

The notes that follow are based on Chapter 9 of *Our Faith Story* by Patrick Purnell (Collins, 1985).

COMPANIONSHIP

1. We all feel a fundamental need for other people. There are many ways in which this need can be expressed and fulfilled: most often by being with others in a shared activity of some kind, e.g. sport, hobbies, interests, being members of the same club, family life, etc.

2. The heart of companionship lies in the way we find ourselves accepted:
- we are able to be ourselves;
- we are valued for what we are;
- we share what is important, both joys and problems.

Together, we build one another up.

3. In companionship, we
- show our need for one another;
- overcome loneliness and fulfil our need for others;
- receive a sense of belonging, personal significance and value;
- are able to grow as people in all areas of our lives;
- are able to build others up, because we feel loved and cared for.

COMMUNITY

Companionship is at the heart of community.

We can measure the extent to which we have achieved community by examining the quality of the relationships that exist among us, and how we function as a body.

There are two possible harmful extremes in people coming together:

>they can come together in order to do something that will benefit each one, but merely tolerating each other in order to achieve it;

>or, they can form an elite group that is very inward looking, held together by an unhealthy love which keeps everyone else out.

'BASIC COMMUNITIES'

'Basic communities' are another expression of communities, to be found in increasing numbers in the developing world. In these basic communities the people, mainly poor, and with little if any education, gather together to reflect upon their experience of life in the light of the Gospel. In so doing they encourage and support each other in their struggle to deal with their terrible living conditions. It may seem that there is very little that they can change. But what they can achieve is a sense of their own worth and dignity as people. Together, they share whatever they do have; above all they share one another's suffering. They are signs of hope to each other.

Beginnings

The first Basic Christian Community, or Base Community as they are sometimes called, began in Brazil in 1956. Their history is told by the Brazilian theologian José Marins:

>The Bishop of the Brazilian diocese of Barra do Pirai was visiting the home town of an old woman who complained to him '. . . at Christmas, the three Protestant churches were lit up and crowded. We could hear their hymn-singing . . . and our Catholic church was in darkness . . . because we could not get a priest.'

This brought home to the Bishop the serious situation the Catholic Church was in if everything had to stop due to a lack of priests, especially since he knew how scarce priests were likely to become throughout his diocese.

What would become of the Church? Who would instruct the people and organize the worship?

In a bold attempt to answer these fundamental questions, the 'people's catechists' were formed; they were trained, taught how to teach and organize the local communities in the name of their bishop. By the end of 1956 there were some 372 such catechists.

Building the whole person

Because the majority of people in Brazil are poor, the work of the catechists could not be concerned simply with the spiritual growth of the people; circumstances demanded initiatives in the sphere of education, of health care, of raising of social awareness. Gifted and knowledgeable people from within the communities emerged to offer leadership.

NEW COMMUNITIES

All over Brazil, a new way of being a church community was growing. Small groups of people gathered together to reflect on the scriptures, to pray together, and to reflect on their everyday lives. Their religion was not something to be practised once a week in some special building, but it became something at the heart of everything they did.

Because they were Christians, they had to respond to each other as such: 'we live and work together as community because we are Christians'.

After the Second Vatican Council, basic Christian communities grew all over Brazil; Pope Paul VI described them as 'the hope of the Church' (*Evangelization in the Modern World*).

Today there are an estimated 150,000 people living in basic Christian communities in Brazil. They are now spreading throughout the developing world. (*Tomorrow's Parish* by Adrian B. Smith, published by McCrimmon Publishing, is a booklet which explores how ideas from these basic Christian communities might be applied in Great Britain.)

THE PARISH

Originally, parishes were Christian communities. Nowadays, it is very difficult to see how parishes can be communities in the true sense of the word. At best, they are a loose gathering of many different groups of people, based around a geographical area.

The eucharist is the true sign of community. It is the celebration of the Body of the Lord, whose prime meaning and manifestation is the Church; they gather around the Lord's table to share and so to become one body, filled with the Spirit.

It is a sign of what they are striving to become, but as yet have not achieved fully. It does not follow that those who gather round the same altar are necessarily a true community. Very often the very size of the group gathered together, and the jumble of motives they may have for being there, do not help make it a place where everyone can feel a sense of acceptance, caring, affirmation.

In the midst of this, the eucharist serves as a call to God's pilgrim people to be a community, and at the same time enables them to become that community

Community is something which is felt rather than defined.

True community always leads to action for the community and for those outside the community.

DISCUSSION TOPICS
Unit 3 Session 1

Talk over the following with a friend:

Do you feel that you need other people?
How well do you think you relate to others?
Do you value your friendships because of what
you can get out of them? or because of what
you are able to give? a bit of both?
What for you makes friendship important?
Do you feel the need to belong to a group?

What do you think of the 'basic
Christian communities' idea?
Do you think it would be possible
in this country? in your parish?
Could you be part of such a group?

When you last went to your parish church for Mass:
- were you made to feel welcome?
- did anyone make an effort to speak to you?
- was it an experience you would want to repeat?
- did you help to make others welcome?

What groups or organizations
are there in your parish?
Can anyone join?
Are you in any parish group?
which one, and why?

Would you describe your parish as 'lively'?
Where should the 'life' of a parish come from?
Are you able to contribute to the 'life' of your parish?

From SEARCH FOR MEANING, published by Geoffrey Chapman, © Judith Russi SSMN 1990.
Multiple copies may be made only by the institution which has purchased a master set.

UNIT 3
SESSION 2
THE SCHOOL OR COLLEGE AS COMMUNITY*

*If the programme is being used in a parish-based setting, then:
> either relate back to the students' experiences when they were at school,
> or adapt the ideas presented here to apply to the students' current circumstances.

This session builds on the groundwork established in the first session. That is, having reached a clearer understanding of what 'community' means, we apply this to the students' own experience.

Is it possible for this school to be a community? Here are some basic questions which should help test this:

> What is the total number of people in the school?
> Do we know them all?
> How do we treat younger pupils?
> How do we treat the teaching staff?
> How do we treat the domestic/administrative staff?
> How do we treat members of the opposite sex?
> How do we treat visitors to the school?

Deeper than these, we need to question the aims and objectives of the school:

> Can we honestly say that the aim of this school, in all that it does, is to help everyone connected with it feel valued, cared about, loved, accepted and affirmed?
> What measures exist within the school to try and achieve this kind of aim? (Year groups? House system? Tutor groups? etc.)

'Community' begins to happen when everyone contributes to the building up of that group. Encourage the students to reflect on what their individual role or contribution should be. Look together at school life, and identify what its needs are. Thereafter, we need to decide what we are going to do about it.

DISCUSSION TOPICS
Unit 3 Session 2

Discuss the following in groups:

*How well do you get on
with those you work beside?
Try and give reasons.*

*What do you think
would help create
a greater sense of community
in your place of work?*

*How well do you get on with
those who are 'below' you?*

*How do they think
they see you?*

*Are there any ways you could
help make things more of a
community for them?*

*How well do you get on
with your superiors,
with those 'above' you?
Do you ever meet for social
events? A meal or a coffee
break together?
If it has not happened till now,
might it be possible
in the future?
Do you think it would help?*

UNIT 3
SESSIONS 3, 4 AND 5

Here are a number of suggestions for 'community' related activities. They are only suggestions, and groups must determine what they can realistically undertake.

The aim is over the next three weeks to introduce the students to as many different ways as possible of discovering 'community', both within the school or parish, and in reaching out to others in the wider community.

If the programme is being followed in school, it may not be possible for the students to leave the school premises during the time allocated to religious education. Instead, the religious education time might be used to plan and prepare for such external visits (the handout of extracts from real-life cases should be useful for such preparatory work); or, it might be used to bring in groups to visit the school.

ACTIVITIES WITHIN THE SCHOOL/PARISH

1. School: Working with children who need extra help.

   Parish: Working with adult literacy classes.

This can be very rewarding for both parties. Basically, it is a case of being aware of people who may be having difficulty with their work, and of offering some of our time and skills to help them. In school this may be helping pupils lower down the school, whether at lunchtime or after school; if the students are already working, there may be some of their colleagues that they could help improve their literacy or numeracy.

2. Open house

Encourage the students to remember when they were new to a situation: first day at school, first day at work, etc. They could now help others who are in those circumstances.

School: invite new pupils to the school to visit the sixth form. Perhaps the first-year pupils can have a sixth former allocated to them, who will take a special interest in them.

Parish: invite young adults who are new to the area to visit your group.

3. A prayer group

Establish a time, and possibly but not necessarily a place, where all those who want can come together for moments of prayer. This prayer might focus on the needs of the community: for those who are sick; thanksgiving for something; etc.

4. Hospitality

The welcome that visitors are offered, whether at school, in the parish or at work, is very important. Encourage the students to take the initiative in keeping the main entrance tidy, welcoming and interesting.

5. Bringing people into our community

Organize a coffee morning, especially for people who may be living alone and might not be able to get out of the house very often. (In the school situation, enlist the help of members of staff and parents to help with transport.)

Or organize a 'mothers and toddlers' session: provide tea and refreshments, and look after the children while the mothers have a chance for some adult conversation with each other!

6. Former pupils/group members/employees

It is important to keep in touch with former colleagues, so that they feel cared about. This might be specially welcome to those who are out of work. Arrange for them to visit for coffee and a chat. Explore what other ways there might be in which your group could help them.

7. Home visits

Establish a list of housebound people, and arrange to visit and befriend them.

ACTIVITIES IN THE WIDER COMMUNITY

There is a certain presumption that because we live in a welfare state, we have social services, and because there are a number of professionally organized voluntary agencies, that we don't really need to offer any more help.

This is false. In fact, most of these agencies could not function at all without the voluntary help of ordinary people. Apart from that, there are many who would welcome help, but find they are not eligible for official help, or perhaps there is no organization that addresses their particular need. Others again, especially the elderly, fight shy of official help, for whatever reasons.

There are, then, needs that the students may well be able to help answer. Undertaking this work is not only important for their own development, but is very much appreciated by those whom they help. You may find it helpful to use the handout of extracts from real-life situations to help persuade the students of the worth of the help they offer, however insignificant it may seem.

The first practical stage is to compile a list of the agencies that are active in your area, and contact them to find out what help is needed. Thereafter, have the students plan their activity, on the basis that they try and match the needs to their aptitudes. Take care, though, because some of the tasks will seem more 'interesting' or 'exciting' (e.g. the idea of being a disc jockey for a hospital radio) than others. Encourage them to value the tasks in terms of the usefulness to those they help.

Here is a basic list of the kind of agencies you will most probably find have branches in most counties:

1. Care Scheme

This is a project for helping all people in need. It covers a very wide range of activities, such that any able-bodied person is able to help in some way.

2. Community Health Councils

Run support schemes for the mentally handicapped.

3. Community Service Volunteers

Offers opportunity for young people to work for a year with a community organization.

4. Community Youth Centres

Can be contacted through the local Social Services Department.

5. Councils for Voluntary Service

Their work is to co-ordinate the voluntary work in the area. Can be contacted through the local Social Services Department.

6. Fish Scheme

Christian based scheme, run by local Council of Churches. Again, a wide range of activities.

7. Hospitals

Many hospitals operate a 'Friends of the Hospital' scheme, part of which is often the hospital radio.

8. Volunteer Bureau

Similar to 1. above; can be contacted through the local Social Services Department.

9. WRVS

Works on a friend-to-friend basis.

10. Youth groups

There is always a need for volunteers to work with young people. Many of these are church or parish based. Be prepared to approach and help youth groups organized by denominations other than your own.

DISCUSSION RESOURCES
Unit 3 Sessions 3-5

From a care worker's notebook:

I had occasion recently to visit all the schools in my
own town to help spread the work of Help the Aged.
The first school was on the outskirts of town. I
arived quite early and parked my car near the main
entrance. I pushed open the front door, only to find
my hand had unearthed someone's recently discarded
chewing-gum stuck onto the handle. Not very pleasant!
I reported to the secretary, as instructed, and was
told to take a seat until the Head was free. This gave
me a good opportunity to take stock. I was not
impressed with what I saw. The magazines on the table
were tatty and old, as were the displays on the wall.
Graffiti adorned one excellent drawing of an old man
looking out of his window. I wondered what the young
artist felt like as he saw his hard work treated in
this way. The whole entrance had a seedy, unwelcoming
look about it. There was a pile of old boxes in one
corner which had obviously been there for ages. A
school bag lay open by the wall alongside an old
tennis racket. A faded rug of dubious origin lay in
the centre, and an elderly, rather sick rubber plant
sadly drooped its leaves in the corner. Now first
impressions count, and my first impression - rightly
or wrongly - was of a school which cared neither for
its visitors nor for itself. I began to wonder how
interested they would be in my work for the old
people. If they cared so little for themselves, how
much would they care for other people?

From a doctor's note-book:

TUESDAY 7th
Called on old Mr S . . . again this morning. Seemed depressed. Whole conversation revolves around tablets. He needs most of them, could do without some, but seems determined to get into the Guinness Book of Records! Well, if it stops his depression, it's worth it. Increased the depression tabs.

FRIDAY 10th
Mr S . . .'s daughter rang. Father worse. Called after lunch. Very depressed. Talked about ending it all. Don't suppose he will, but must keep an eye on the situation. Insisted daughter kept all tablets, and give only what I prescribed.

MONDAY 13th
Called to see Mr S . . . Little change. Daughter said she'd call if there was a problem. She's monitoring tablets well.

THURSDAY 30th
Not heard from Mr S . . . for some time, so called in. Couldn't believe my eyes. He was up and dressed. Was glad to see me, but hoped I wouldn't stay long as he was expecting a visitor. Daughter told me that a lad nearby heard Mr S . . . had been in the Navy so asked to see him. She was rather concerned but let him come. Worked a treat. They are now good friends, They were chatting about sea, and travelling. When I left he was sorting out old photos of his time at sea. It was obviously people not pills he needed. No sign of depression. Now able to stop many of his tablets.

DISCUSSION RESOURCES
Unit 3   Sessions 3 - 5

From a parish newsletter:

> Mr J ███████ needs someone to help tidy his garden. He is recovering well from his operation but is not able to lift anything or to bend yet.
>
> Two very elderly ladies have been in the geriatric ward for over two years and now get very few visitors. They would welcome short visits at any time.
>
> The Special School in Taylors Road ugently needs help in repairing toys and educational equipment.
>
> Young mother who has unfortunately broken her leg would be glad if someone could take her five year old son to school each morning. His father can pick him up after school.
>
> If you can help any of these people, please phone 583672 as soon as possible.

From the letters page of a local newspaper:

Dear Sir,
On behalf of my neighbour who is over 80 I would like to publicly say thank you to the pupils of ███████ School for the way in which they entertained 100 elderly people last Thursday afternoon. All the guests had a wonderful time. They were warmly welcomed at the door, given a splendid tea and entertained by the pupils. Many of these people do not live in special homes where such invitations are quite frequent, but live alone with son or daughter and are often overlooked when food parcels and invitations are given out. So it is very much to the school's credit that they managed to find the addresses of these lonely people, many of whom had not been out for a long time. I would also like to thank the staff who kindly used their cars to collect and return the guests. All who attended the party now have something to talk about for weeks to come and look forward to the party promised for next year.

'Religion is a private matter
between the individual and God.
Notions like "community"
are figments of the pious imagination
of those who don't have enough to do.'

'Schools are established
to offer young people the opportunity
to acquire a sound academic education
that will enable them
to secure a good job
and hold their own
in the market-place of society.'

'In the light of cuts in the social services
and National Health Service,
it makes good economic sense
to close down the big institutions
and to integrate people
back into the community,
where they can be taken care of
by the local community.'

UNIT 4
SESSION 1
JUSTICE AND PEACE BEGIN HERE

1. We are living in an age where there is greater awareness of the suffering and injustice that exist in our world. Examples of this would be: Live Aid and the Ethiopian famine; the AIDS campaigns.

2. This is not solely a case of being better informed; there seems to be a greater social conscience nowadays. People seem aware that the whole area of social inequality and injustice is the responsibility of each one of us. For example, excuses like these are heard less often nowadays:
    - 'I didn't cause the famine';
    - 'It's nothing to do with me';
    - 'If they worked harder they wouldn't be in trouble'.

3. However, the sheer scale of some of the problems often leaves people feeling powerless to do anything about it. For example, how can any one person do anything about vast economic inequities? Or in the face of overwhelming political forces? Or because of cultural restrictions? For some of us, looking on through our television sets, we may be so overwhelmed that we 'switch off'.

4. A sense of history may help combat such pessimism. History is full of examples of people inflicting injustices on others (slavery, for example); but equally history shows us people who have worked to overcome these same injustices and sufferings (William Wilberforce; Abraham Lincoln).

5. The people who, throughout history, have worked for human rights began life in much the same way as their contemporaries;

88

they grew up as children in the world, became part of their local community. The difference came when they became socially aware of what was happening around them, and opted to do something about it.

6. Martin Luther King Jr was not born as a civil rights leader; he became one because of the way he saw his black brothers and sisters being treated. Bob Geldof was not born as a famine-fighting fund-raiser; suddenly prompted by what he saw on television, he decided to do what he could.

7. Christians believe that any freely chosen attack on a person or any violation of another's human rights is sinful; it is an act against God and his kingdom.

8. What can we do?
8.1   The first step is to be aware of the nature and extent of injustices in our own area.
8.2   The second step is to research and analyse the situation and circumstances. The key questions to ask are:
- who?
- what?
- where?
- why?
- how?
8.3   This clarifies the injustice, and equally should clarify what steps are appropriate in combating it.

Key subjects in this area are sexism and racism, and this unit should feature a session on at least one of these topics. Resource materials are available, free, from organizations such as CAFOD and Christian Aid: this includes the usual range of pamphlets, posters, etc., but in addition they can provide speakers on these topics.

9. Beyond identifying injustices inflicted by others, we need to become aware of injustices in which we ourselves may be implicitly involved. Although we may not be involved individually, we may be partly responsible by being a member of a society that is behaving unjustly. Once we have identified an

injustice, we may have to face up to the fact that we are part of a society or a group within society that is inflicting that injustice. Facing up to it means we must act to remedy the injustice.

For example, someone may belong to a group for reasons to do with sport or music; it may happen that this group may promote racial hatred (e.g. a golf club which will not accept Jewish members; football supporters who use racist chants or who attack fans of other nationalities). Although you yourself may not have expressed it personally, by belonging to the group you are identified with that attitude.

10. As Christians we believe we have the Word of God entrusted to us in the scriptures; that Word is full of calls for social justice. Jesus clearly identified himself with the poor and the oppressed, and insisted that anyone who wanted to claim to be his follower had to respond to the cry of the poor.

Has there been any event connected with *Justice* and *Peace* in which you have taken part in the past year or so?
In small groups discuss what the event was, and why you became involved;
or, explain your reasons for not getting involved.

This is the Pastoral Cycle Method which is used by the basic Christian communities:

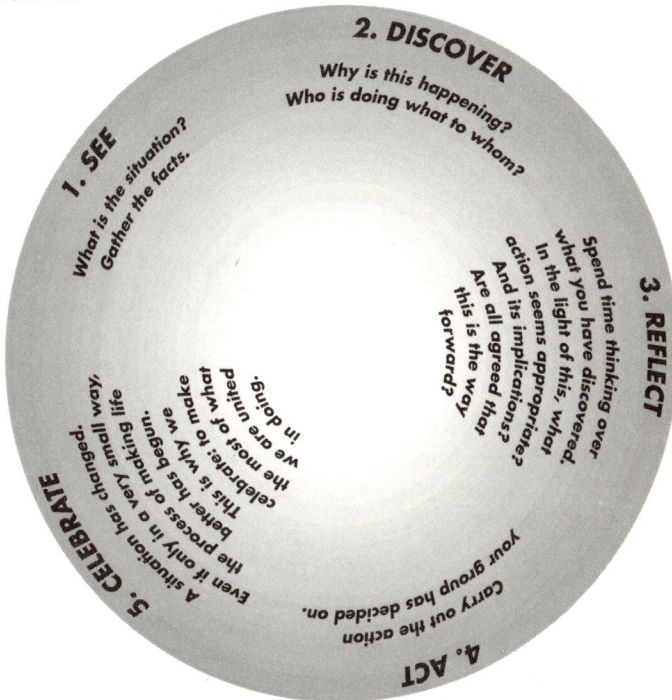

2. DISCOVER
Why is this happening?
Who is doing what to whom?

1. SEE
What is the situation?
Gather the facts.

3. REFLECT
Spend time thinking over what you have discovered. In the light of this, what action seems appropriate? And its implications? Are all agreed that this is the way forward?

4. ACT
Carry out the action your group has decided on.

5. CELEBRATE
A situation has changed. Even if only in a very small way. This is why we celebrate; to make the most of what better has begun. the process of making life we are doing.

Apply this to your lifestyle. Here are some key questions:
  - are there people who you feel do not have the same opportunities as you and your group?
  - are there ways in which they are not given the respect they should be?
  - are there ways in which they are treated unjustly by other young people/students?

(It's unlikely you'll complete all parts of the method in the time allocated to the session. Carry the process on as best you can beyond the session.)

UNIT 4
SESSION 2
JESUS AND JUSTICE AND PEACE

1. The Gospels are full of Jesus' concern for the outcasts of society. He knew that the poor, the hungry, the sick, the blind, the lame, the underprivileged, slaves, widows and orphans were discriminated against; they were often deprived of their rights, made to feel they were a blight on society, and barely tolerated. Jesus saw them cheated, mistreated, abused, and put upon by those who had economic and political control over them. Jesus regarded everyone as a child of the same heavenly Father, and entitled to be treated with respect and dignity. So it is we find Jesus spending his life preaching and acting against injustice and suffering.

2. Jesus went first to those who were most in need: they were the 'outsiders'; the 'unclean'; the 'despised'; the 'expendable'. Because they were without power, influence or money, they were very much second-class citizens. They were kept in economic and political bondage by the ruling class, who regarded the poor's sufferings as punishment for their sins. For the poor in the time of Jesus there must have seemed no way out.

3. Jesus came to people such as these as a sign of hope. Jesus taught them that in God's eyes they were equal to the most wealthy and powerful on earth; that God loved them as his children; that they had a dignity that no one could take from them. Jesus gave them hope by preaching against the evils current in society, and the injustices and oppression that kept the weak downtrodden and powerless. Jesus demanded that those who had wealth should share with the poor.

4. Jesus said,
'When you give something to a needy person, do not make a big show of it, as the hypocrites do in the houses of worship and on the streets. They do it so that people will praise them. I assure you, they have already been paid in full.

'But when you help a needy person, do it in such a way that even your closest friend will not know about it. Then it will be a private matter. And your Father, who sees what you do in private, will reward you.'
Matthew 6:2-4 (*Good News Bible*)

5. Jesus knew that as long as there were inequities in society, as long as there were 'haves' and 'have nots', as long as people were excluded from their rightful place in society, as long as there were exploiters and exploited, then people would not be able to live in the peace that God intended for them, nor could they grow fully into being the men and women that God had created them to be.

6. We are created in love and for love; we long to live in peace. This is what God intended for us, which Jesus encourages us to rediscover. Jesus' own life is a symbol, a witness to what could be for all human beings.

DISCUSSION TOPICS
Unit 4 Session 2

Divide into small groups and discuss:

In today's society who would
you say are 'outsiders';
'unclean'; 'despised';
expendable?
How have these people come to
be thought of in this way?
Do you know anyone who
would fall into any of these
groups?

How do you think
these people feel about
being treated in this way?
How might you feel
in their place?

What do you think is meant by
'the North-South divide'?
How do you feel about it?

ROLE PLAY

Characters: A group of four: three friends
and a newcomer.
The newcomer is badly
handicapped, and as result
dribbles, and can barely
speak. He/she walks with
crutches. He/she has come
to this school/college
because the special school can
no longer provide adequate
facilities for this person, who
has a very high IQ.
The newcomer is not very
long there before one person
starts to make fun of him/her.
Another person starts to argue that 'people like that
shouldn't be in a normal school/college'.

Role play: Act out how the three friends deal with the situation.

Do you think it's possible to bring about a world that fits the scriptural
vision of 'the kingdom of God'?

From SEARCH FOR MEANING, published by Geoffrey Chapman, © Judith Russi SSMN 1990.
Multiple copies may be made only by the institution which has purchased a master set.

UNIT 4
SESSION 3
THE CHURCH - FACING THE CHALLENGE

1. 'Never before have people possessed such great potential for achieving the goals of civilization, and never before has such civilization been so seriously threatened with local, national, or global destruction. On the one hand, people have the tools to eliminate the evils that threaten humanity. On the other hand, they have the means to destroy what people have so painstakingly built for thousands of years. . .'

2. '. . . The gap between rich and poor is perhaps the most pressing problem of our day. The nations that enjoy sufficiency and abundance of everything may not overlook the plight of other nations whose citizens experience such domestic problems that they are all but overcome by poverty and hunger, and are not able to enjoy human rights.'
Pope John XXIII, *Mater et Magistra* (1961).

3. The body of Christians, called the Church, is a social organization. As such it has the same obligations as does an individual in witnessing to the need for a just and peaceful world. It does so by exerting its spiritual, moral, and ecclesiastical force in the political and economic world in which we live.

POLITICAL REALM
4. Although the Church is not first and foremost a political institution, it does have a certain political power due to the sheer size of its membership. Church members, as citizens of the body politic, can and should act *en bloc* to influence official legislation or unofficial customs.

In democratic societies, various denominations and religious groupings can act as a lobby to bring about change.

PROPHETIC REALM

5. Sometimes it is necessary for the Church to speak out, both from the pulpit and in the world (through the media) on important moral issues and implications which have political consequences. When the whole Christian Church co-operates across the denominational differences, then the impact is even greater.

6. In countries where freedom of expression is limited, or the country is ruled by whatever form of dictatorship, the Church cannot exercise the same kind of political power. Instead it can witness to the need for change. This witness can be dangerous: it may lead to imprisonment, torture and even death. It is essential that the Church does not shy away from the task of this particular form of witness.

7. The Church also fulfils its prophetic role by documents and pronouncements which reaffirm Christ's teaching on justice and peace, and interpret it for the contemporary world:

'In his actions Jesus showed the way of living in God's reign; he manifested the forgiveness which he called for when he accepted all who came to him, forgave their sins, healed them, released them from demons who possessed them. In doing these things, he made the tender mercy of God present in a world which knew violence, oppression and injustice. Jesus pointed out the injustices of his time and opposed those who laid burdens upon the people or defiled true worship. He acted aggressively and dramatically at times, as when he cleansed the Temple of those who had made God's house into a "den of robbers".'

The Challenge of Peace, 48
Pastoral Letter by the Bishops' Conference of the United States

8. 'Confronted by this economic complexity and seeking clarity for the future, we can rightly ask ourselves one single question: how does our economic system affect the lives of people - all people? Part of the American dream has been to make this world a better place for people to live in: at this moment in history that dream must include everyone on this globe. Since we profess to be members of a "catholic" or universal religion,

we must raise our sights to a concern for the well-being of everyone in the world. Third World debt becomes our problem. Famine and starvation in sub-Saharan Africa becomes our concern. Rising military expenditures everywhere in the world become part of our fears for the future of this planet. We cannot be content if we see ecological neglect or squandering of natural resources. In this letter, we Bishops have spoken often of economic interdependence: now is the moment when all of us must confront the reality of such economic bonding and its consequences, and see it as a moment of grace - a *kairos* – that can unite all of us in a common community of the human family. We commit ourselves to this global vision.'

Economic Justice for All, 363

Pastoral Letter by the Bishops' Conference of the United States

9. 'Since all men and women are members of the same human family, they are indissolubly linked with one another in the one destiny of the whole world, in the responsibility for which they all share . . . action on behalf of justice and participation in the transformation of the world . . . appear to us as a constitutive dimension of the Gospel, or, in other words, of the Church's mission for the redemption of the human race and its liberation from every oppressive situation.'

Justice in the World

Document of the 1971 General Assembly of the World Synod of Bishops

10. These are the main recent documents of the Church which deal with the concerns of social justice:

Rerum Novarum (1891)
Encyclical Letter by Pope Leo XIII on the condition of labour.
Quadragesimo Anno (1931)
Encyclical Letter by Pope Pius XI marking the 40th anniversary of *Rerum Novarum*, on reconstructing the social order.
Mater et Magistra (1961)
Encyclical Letter of Pope John XXIII on Christianity and social progress, attacking the unequal distribution of the world's wealth and resources.

Pacem in Terris (1963)

Encyclical Letter of Pope John XXIII on peace, poverty and human rights as issues that call for committed action by Christians.

Gaudium et Spes (1965)

Pastoral Constitution on The Church in the Modern World (Vatican II) on Christian people's responsibility for the world and the human condition.

Populorum Progressio (1967)

Encyclical Letter of Pope Paul VI on the condition of Third World peoples and how Communism and capitalism relate to their development.

Octogesimo Adveniens (1971)

Encyclical Letter of Pope Paul VI, marking the 80th anniversary of *Rerum Novarum* (see above); a call to political action for world justice and peace.

Justice in the World (1971)

Declaration of the Second General Assembly of the World Synod of Bishops; a call to act for justice and to participate in transforming the world as constitutive dimensions of being faithful to the Gospel.

Evangelii Nuntiandi (1975)

Encyclical Letter of Paul VI on how the Gospel relates to today's world.

Redemptor Hominis (1979)

Encyclical Letter of Pope John Paul II on the state of contemporary society.

Laborem Exercens (1981)

Encyclical Letter of Pope John Paul II on the value of labour, of human work.

The Challenge of Peace: God's promise and our response (1983)

Pastoral Letter of the Catholic Bishops' Conference of the United States on the Church's teaching on peace, on war; a call to Christians to be peacemakers.

Economic Justice for All: Catholic social teaching and the US economy (1986)

Pastoral Letter of the Catholic Bishops' Conference of the United States; a call to transform the US economic policy for the benefit of all people, especially the poor and the homeless.

PRIESTLY ROLE

11. The Church also serves the world by prayer. Prayer that God's kingdom will come on earth, as in heaven; prayer for the poor and dispossessed; prayer for those who oppress and cause the suffering; the prayer of the countless million individuals; by the corporate prayer of the Church, the liturgy.

From the *Eucharistic Prayer for Masses of Reconciliation II*:
'Father, all powerful and ever living God,
we praise and thank you
through Jesus Christ our Lord
for your presence and action in the world.
In the midst of conflict and division,
we know it is you who turn our minds to thoughts of
    peace.
Your Spirit changes our hearts:
enemies begin to speak to one another,
those who were estranged join hands in friendship,
and nations seek the way of peace together.
Your Spirit is at work:
when understanding puts an end to strife,
when hatred is quenched by mercy,
and vengeance gives way to forgiveness.
. . .
God of power and might,
we praise you through your Son, Jesus Christ,
who comes in your name.
He is the Word that brings salvation.
He is the hand you stretch out to sinners.
He is the way that leads to your peace.
God our Father,
we had wandered far away from you,
but through your Son you have brought us back.
You gave him up to death
so that we might turn again to you
and find our way to one another.
Therefore we celebrate the reconciliation
Christ has gained for us.
. . .
Fill us with his Spirit through our sharing in this meal.
May he take away all that divides us.
. . .

Father, make your Church throughout the world
a sign of unity and an instrument of your peace.
. . .
In that new world
where the fullness of your peace will be revealed,
gather people of every race, language, and way of life
to share in the one eternal banquet
with Jesus Christ the Lord.'

12. 'It is one thing to free the oppressed.
    It is quite another to free the oppressor.'
A. Bredin, *Disturbing the Peace* (Fowler Wright, 1986)

DISCUSSION TOPICS
Unit 4 Session 3

Discuss the following
with a friend:

In some countries, priests and bishops
speak out boldly for peace and justice.
Some have even gone to gaol as a result.
In other countries, clergy who speak out
are accused of 'meddling in politics'.
What are your thoughts on this?

Discuss this in
small groups:

What does it mean to say that the
Church has a prophetic mission?
How, in your opinion, should the Church
fulfill this role in practice?
Who is it that has to be 'prophetic'?
Offer suggestions at international,
national and local levels.

Once you have discussed these
amongst yourselves, arrange to meet
with your local clergy, perhaps for
coffee, and discuss your views about
the Church with them.
You might do the same with local
politicians.

From SEARCH FOR MEANING, published by Geoffrey Chapman, © Judith Russi SSMN 1990.
Multiple copies may be made only by the institution which has purchased a master set.

UNIT 4
SESSION 4
IMAGINE A PEACEFUL WORLD

1. John Lennon was asked during an interview why he devoted so much time and energy to peace. Wasn't it a waste of time? Lennon replied that he believed that it was Leonardo da Vinci who made flying possible by projecting it, by bringing it into people's consciousness as even a possibility.

'What a person projects can eventually happen', Lennon said, 'and therefore I always want to project peace. I want to project it in song, in word, in action. I want to put the possibility of peace into the public imagination, and I know as certain as I am standing here, I know that someday peace will be.'

2. In our efforts to work for peace and justice we may overlook the power of imagination, of hope, of dreaming, of faith. These do not replace other work for peace and justice, but they underpin such work. And if everyone shared the same dream . . .

'You may say I'm a dreamer,
but I'm not the only one.'
John Lennon, *Imagine*.

3. 'Nothing could be worse than fear that one has given up too soon and left one effort unexpended which might have saved the world.'
Jane Addams, Nobel Peace Prize Winner 1931.

4. 'Because of our faith in Jesus Christ and in humankind, we must apply our humble efforts to the construction of a more just and humane world. And I want to declare emphatically: that such a world is possible. To create this new society, we must present outstretched, friendly hands, without hatred, without rancour - even as we show great determination, never waver-

ing in the defence of truth and justice, because we know that seeds are not sown with clenched fists. To sow we must open our hands.'
Adolfo Pérez Esquivel, Nobel Peace Prize Winner 1980.

5. When we look at the war torn parts of the world, even to dream of peace may seem impossible. Yet history constantly reminds us that it has often been from the seemingly weakest sources that a great force for peace has sprung.

Kurt Kauter illustrates this well with a little fable:
'Tell me the weight of a snowflake', a coal-tit asked a wild dove.
'Nothing more than nothing', was the answer.
'In that case, I must tell you a marvellous story', the coal-tit said. 'I sat on a branch of a fir, close to its trunk, when it began to snow. Not heavily, not in a raging blizzard. No, just like in a dream, without a sound and without any violence. Since I did not have anything better to do, I counted the snowflakes settling on the twigs and needles of my branch. There were exactly 3,741,952. When the 3,741,953rd dropped onto the branch - nothing more than nothing as you say - the branch broke off.'
Having said that, the coal-tit flew away.
The dove, since Noah's time an authority on the matter, thought about the story for a while and finally said to herself,
'Perhaps there is only one person's voice lacking for peace to come to the world.'

6. Gandhi once said,
'The only people on earth who do not see Christ and his teachings as non-violent are Christians.'

Where do we stand in our commitment to peace?

DISCUSSION TOPICS
Unit 4 Session 4a

Can you imagine a peaceful world?
Share your ideas with a friend.

What are some of the things that prevent peace?
- at home?
- at school?
- after school, with friends?
- at work?

Mark this list from 1 to 10 according to those which you think could be prevented most easily:

	parent hits child
	civilians are bombed in wartime
	a prisoner in Northern Ireland is tortured by the police or by the army to extract information
	a woman stabs and kills her husband after years of being beaten by him
	South African students riot and smash the windows of white owned shops
	a fight in the sixth form block over music
	a black student is continually called 'nigger' by a group of students
	rioting by unemployed people in the North of England
	football supporters smash up a train
	a teenage gang put a fire bomb through the letter box of an elderly person's home

In small groups, compare and discuss your ratings.

Do you think the media help or hinder the cause for peace?

I have a dream
that one day this nation will rise up
and live out the true meaning of the creed:
'We hold these truths to be self-evident,
that all men are created equal.'

I have a dream
that one day on the red hills of Georgia
the sons of former slaves and the sons of former slave-owners
will be able to sit down together at the table of brotherhood.

I have a dream
that even the state of Mississippi, a desert state
sweltering with the heat of injustice and oppression,
will be transformed into an oasis of freedom and justice.

I have a dream
that one day my four children will live in a nation
where they will not be judged by the colour of their skin
but by the content of their character.

I have a dream today . . .

I have a dream
that one day every valley shall be exalted,
every hill and mountain shall be made low;
the rough places will be made plain,
and the crooked places will be made straight,
and the glory of the Lord shall be revealed,
and all flesh shall see it together.

This is our hope.
This is the faith with which I return to the South.
With this faith we will be able to hew
out of the mountain of despair a stone of hope.
With this we will be able to transform
the jangling discords of our nation
into a beautiful symphony of brotherhood.

With this faith we will be able to work together,
to pray together, to go to jail together,
knowing that we will be free one day . . .

**This is a famous speech, not just because of the beauty of Martin Luther
King's words, but for the power of the vision that it offers.
What do you notice about the faith that this speech expresses?
What other qualities does it inspire?**

UNIT 4
SESSION 5
IF YOU WANT PEACE, WORK FOR JUSTICE

The aim of this session is to introduce the students to what is already being done in the field of human rights, peace and justice. Materials are available from Diocesan Peace and Justice Offices, from Justice and Peace Centres, or from the main agencies (addresses below).

1. Peace and justice are inextricably linked. We may long for peace, but it will remain an impossibility as long as there are people all over the world suffering injustices of every kind. If we want peace, we must work for justice.

2. The task is a vast one, and certainly too big for one person. Hence the need to know what is already being done. By joining with others, by sharing our dreams, we can achieve the seemingly impossible.

3. For this session it is probably most helpful to invite a speaker from CAFOD, SCIAF or Trocaire; or CIIR; or Pax Christi; or Amnesty International; or Christian CND, etc. to come and speak to the students about their work. At the very least, write to the following agencies for information and prepare a display. The key objective of this session is to let the students see what is already being done, and hopefully ways in which they can do something.

Amnesty International, British Section, 5 Roberts Place, London EC1 0EJ. Tel: 071 251 8371

CAFOD, 2 Romero Close, Stockwell Road, London SW9 9TY. Tel: 071 733 7900

Christian Action, St Peter's House, 308 Kennington Lane, London SE11 5HY. Tel: 071 735 2372

Christian Aid, PO Box 100, London SE1 7RT.

Christian CND:
England: 22-24 Underwood Street, London N1 7JG. Tel: 071 250 4010
Scotland: 420 Sauchiehall Street, Glasgow G2. Tel: 041 331 2878
Wales: 56 Bryn Aeron, Dunvant, Swansea SA2 7UX. Tel: 0792 206617
Eire: 29 Baggot Street, Dublin 2. Tel: 01 613987
Northern Ireland: 15a Hopefield Avenue, Portrush BT56 8LT. Tel: 0265 824456

CIIR, 22 Coleman Fields, London N1 7AF. Tel: 071 354 0883

Pax Christi, Saint Francis of Assisi Centre, Pottery Lane, London W11 4NQ. Tel: 071 727 4609

Peace Tax Campaign, 1a Hollybush Place, London E2 9QX. Tel: 071 739 5088

SCIAF, 5 Oswald Street, Glasgow G1 4QR. Tel: 041 221 4447

Trocaire, 169 Booterstown Avenue, Dublin, Eire.

DISCUSSION TOPICS
Unit 4 Session 5

Although this is a discussion session, it is important to get beyond this stage of thinking and talking, and into involvement.

In small groups, discuss the various sorts of people that you know who are not being treated as they should: e.g.
- the way new pupils at school, new students at college, new apprentices at work, are treated;
- racism;
- bullying;
- girls not being given equal opportunities;
- elderly people in your area at risk;
- homeless people;
- the housebound;
- single parents.

And what might you do to help them? e.g.
- collecting warm blankets, clothes etc., for the homeless;
- company for the lonely;
- writing to political prisoners;
- running a justice and peace group;
- running a newspaper or newsletter about the plight of the poor, e.g. offering information on the implications of the Poll Tax, the Dole restrictions, Housing Act, Education Act, etc.;
- 'adopt' an area of the world where human rights are violated and organize regular exhibitions, debates, etc., to keep people informed;
- invite your local MP to come and take part in a debate on a justice and peace topic.

'Schools should prepare their pupils
to be good citizens,
who will keep the law, work hard
and mind their own business.
In that way, we would all enjoy life
and live in peace.'

'Peace is so important to the world
that we should be ready
to obtain it at any cost.'

'The Gospels were written 2,000 years ago;
therefore they have little to say
to the complex political world
of nuclear deterrence
and global inter-dependence.'

UNIT 5
SESSION 1
THE SPOKEN WORD AND RELATIONSHIPS

HOW WORDS WORK

This first session explores the power of words in relationships; their power to build, or to destroy.

Words are a means, one of our principal means, of communication. They are tools in the relaying of thoughts, ideas, concepts, experiences, images and feelings.

Invite the students to brainstorm about the ways that words can work. Write up single words or short phrases to stand for each of their suggestions. Then divide them into two lists: one of ways in which words work positively; the other, ways in which they work negatively.

Here are some examples:

Words can . . .	Words can . . .
. . . encourage	. . . discourage
. . . create	. . . destroy
. . . build up	. . . break down
. . . convey truth	. . . convey falsehood
. . . give energy	. . . paralyse

Words on their own are neutral. It is the way in which we use them that gives them their power.

Over and above the conventional meaning that words have, we can overlay them with extra meaning, send extra messages, by the way in which we use them. We do this by tone of voice, by emphasis and by expression.

We know that when we ourselves speak we have certain motives. In hearing and listening to others, we try and discern their motivation.

Words play a key role in relationships between people. Words can act as the cement which binds a relationship together; or words can have the opposite effect.

ROLE PLAY: Part 1

Prepare this short role play beforehand.

The characters are a boy and a girl who have never met each other before. The boy is keen to get to know the girl.

He begins to talk to her, politely, asking questions in a gentle and respectful way; making positive remarks about her.

The girl responds first with indifference, then with cheeky and sarcastic answers. Her remarks are negative.

Eventually, the boy leaves.

Invite the students to explore what the characters' words, their conversation, revealed about them.

e.g. that the boy seemed interested in the girl;
that the girl seemed uninterested.

Lead the discussion to analyse the dynamics of the encounter. The girl was invited to respond; she had a choice in how to respond. Her choice was to say, as clearly as she could, 'Get lost!'. In turn, the boy had a choice how to respond to this message. He chose to accept it, and left.

ROLE PLAY: Part 2

The same two characters, and the same basic scenario of the boy interested in the girl.

Again the boy is polite, respectful, positive; again the girl responds negatively. But this time, the boy challenges her every time she is rude or unkind. After a while, the girl can no longer cope with this, and she leaves.

Once again, invite the students to explore what the course of the conversation reveals about the two characters.

Explore the dynamics. It begins the same way, but it seems the choice the boy makes is not to accept the message at face value. He pushes for honesty, wanting to know what prompts these questions. Perhaps he thinks she didn't mean what she said? Perhaps she responds the way she does not out of bitchiness, but because she is annoyed, or even afraid? Perhaps she believes he didn't mean what he was saying?

The girl now has another choice. For whatever reason, she does not like having to answer for her words, and leaves.

DISCUSSION TOPICS
Unit 5 Session 1

Discuss the following in groups of two:

WALLOP!

Share times when words
have hurt you:
- what was it that
caused you pain?
- how long did it take you
to come to terms
with what was said?

In the second role play
we saw someone trying
to show the other
how negative she was being:
- do you think he was right?
- in your experience,
do things like this
happen in real life?

Would you say you have heard more
positive or more negative things said
about you at school/college/work?
- are your faults pointed out
more than your gifts
and your strong points?
- either way, what has been the
effect on you?

ROLE PLAY

Characters: As in the input session, the same boy and girl.

Scenario: This is the next meeting between them after the
dinner scene.
The girl is still intent on ignoring the boy, but he
will not let her. Eventually she agrees to discuss
what happened in their last conversation.

What happens next?

UNIT 5
SESSION 2
THE POWER OF WORDS

The first session explored the power of the word. This session now looks at the way the media exploit that power. Most probably students will have covered this in third/fourth/fifth form. Be aware of this, and build on it, inviting deeper reflection than 'media studies' would demand, encouraging moral analysis.

THE WRITTEN WORD

Invite the students to consider remarks like:

'Of course it's true! I read it in the papers.
Big headline on the front page.'
'You can trust papers like *The Times*, *Observer*,
Guardian to tell the real truth.'
'I know it's true - I read it in the textbook.'

Have the students ever heard anyone say anything like this? Have they themselves ever said anything like this?

If they are honest they will be saying yes, and the discussion leader will probably have to admit to something similar!

This is a strange phenomenon whereby we seem to accord greater credibility to the written word than the spoken word. Perhaps it is because the spoken word just vanishes into the air, but the printed word remains, fixed. It seems more lasting, more durable, and somehow is treated as if it carries more weight.

Another symptom of this is the burning of books because they are 'heretical', 'blasphemous', 'dangerous'.

Do the ideas the book contained become any less true because the book no longer exists (e.g. Galileo writing that the earth revolved round the sun, and not vice versa as was believed in his time)?

TELEVISION AND RADIO

Advertising showers the viewer or listener with words. How

many are true? How many take liberties with the truth?

Encourage the students to give examples of adverts that they think work well; and then to analyse why it might be that they work. How many of them work by deceiving us, however innocently, however humorously?

What about the news? Are news broadcasts any different?

What about the prominence of certain items on the news?

What comes first? What comes last? How much time is given to each item?

Who decides these things? Why?

Are the editors/producers trying to tell us what is important today, and what is less so?

Are all the items 'news' items? What about events that are staged to attract TV news coverage (particularly at election time)?

TALKING POINTS
Various agencies (the UN and others) were warning of the Ethiopian famine before it reached crisis point. Why did it take so long to hit world news?

During the conflict over the Falklands, reporting in Britain was severely restricted. Why was this? Do you think this was justifiable?

Why is it that one murder gets front page headline treatment one week, while another murder a week later may not even get a mention?

How far do we decide for other people what is important for them to hear, and what we think they shouldn't hear?

Is this right? Is this truth? (Explore this through various scenarios: e.g. parents with children; husband or wife with their partner; government and the public.)

'PROPAGANDA'
With the students, come to a working definition of 'propaganda'. Try and establish a basic 'neutral' definition, and then explore when and how it has come to have a certain pejorative significance.

That is, nowadays we usually use 'propaganda' to mean an over-enthusiasm in getting the message across; in going beyond merely presenting the facts to try and persuade; that this persuasion may involve distorting the facts; that it implies using information to promote an ideology.

In the industrialized countries 'information' is a major industry. In 1989 the bill for the British Government's 'advertising' was £150 million. The Government's advertising campaign for the privatization of the water companies cost more than that of Nescafé Gold Blend, Persil, Guinness and Coca-Cola all put together.

There is a fine line dividing getting the message across and putting out political propaganda. Where would the students draw the line?

Isn't it right to try and ensure that a message you think is important should be got across?

Is propaganda only bad when it is harmful? Only when it involves lies and distortion?

What about churches in the way they put across their message?

What is the difference between religious education and propaganda?

BINDING WORDS

Explore the way we use words to express commitment:

> e.g. 'Give me your word . . .';
> 'I promise . . .'.

There is a special degree of commitment, a serious promise, which is legally binding:

> 'I vow . . .'.

In getting married, each partner makes a vow to the other. In religious life, three vows are usually made: poverty, chastity and obedience.

> 'I swear to tell the truth, the whole truth . . .'

Words spoken under oath are a solemn pronouncement to affirm the truth of what is being said, or to pledge the person to a particular course of action. Usually God is invoked as witness. An oath is not just a solemn pronouncement, it is also legally binding.

DISCUSSION TOPICS
Unit 5 Session 2

In what ways are you influenced
by what you read in a
newspaper?

What do you think about the way
in which some newspapers
cover and report on
the private lives of public figures?

SUNSEEKER
HOLIDAYS

In small teams devise an advert
for one of the following:
shampoo; a drink; an insurance
company; a holiday company.
What means are you going to
use to persuade us of the worth
of your product?
Will you lie, if you have to?
Or, at least, how will you
'doctor' things?

Do you think a person's word
is as important today
as it used to be?
Give reasons for your opinion.

Do you think promises/vows
should ever be broken?
In what circumstances would
you say they could be broken?

UNIT 5
SESSION 3
THE CREATIVE WORD

The aim of this session is to develop an appreciation of the creative power of the word. Establish this first at the level of ordinary human life, and then of spiritual life.

Invite the students to recall and to share moments we have experienced in our lives when we have been happy, felt fulfilled, moments of growth; how many of these have been because of words spoken to and about us:

'You've won . . .';
'You're the best . . .';
'I want you to come to dinner . . .';
'You're special to me . . .';
'I like being with you . . .'.

NAMES
Have a book of names and their meanings handy for this part of the session.

In our society we tend to treat names as labels; they just happen to be attached to individuals, but are not usually expected to have any more meaning than that.

Start by writing the name of someone up where all can see it. Ask the group to say what that name, that word, conveys to them. Is it just a word, a label that happens to be attached to a person, or is it something more?

Look up the meaning of the name, and write that up. Now invite the group to say whether they think that person's name 'fits' him/her.

Repeat the exercise, as time permits, with several names.

Perhaps some of the group know what their name means and why it was given to them. Have them talk about it.

In some cultures they still maintain the tradition of names being more descriptive of the person. Since we have lost this, we find the tradition of nicknames.

'WORD' AS THE NAME OF GOD

Read the Prologue to John's Gospel (1:1ff.)

'In the beginning was the Word:
the Word was with God
and the Word was God . . .'

John's Gospel reveals an aspect of God as 'Word'.

Later in the same passage, Jesus is portrayed as that Word:

' . . . the Word was made flesh,
he lived among us' (John 1:14).

Throughout scripture many other 'names' are used for God, especially in the Psalms:

- Shepherd;
- King;
- rock.

These are echoed in the Gospels by Jesus, who also says of God that he is:

- Abba;
- Vine.

And of himself, Jesus says he is:

- the way, the truth, the life;
- the light of the world;
- the gate;
- the resurrection;
- etc.

In biblical culture, names were very important; knowing someone's name implied that you could command them; knowing a person's name implied having power over them.

- see the many examples where God calls individuals by name, often in a vision or in a dream, to entrust some great task to them: Moses (Exodus 3:1ff., especially v. 4); Samuel (1 Samuel 3:1ff., especially vv. 4, 6, 8);

- see the examples where an individual is named, or given a new name: special names are given to the promised child (Isaiah 9:6); Simon becomes Peter (Matthew 16:18); Saul becomes Paul.

- see how, in the second creation account, God brings the animals to man to see what man would call them; man gave names to all the animals (Genesis 2:19-20).

This is also borne out by the reverence with which the Jewish people still treat the name of God, as revealed to Moses. When Moses asks God who he is, he receives the reply YHWH, meaning 'I Am who I Am' (Exodus 3:13-14). As a mark of respect this name was never pronounced by the Jewish people (so much so that we cannot be sure how it was pronounced; the most probable way is 'Yahweh'). To pronounce the name was considered blasphemous, for which the penalty was stoning. This explains why, at the end of John 8, the people take up stones to throw at Jesus; because three times he has said the name of God: 'I am He' 8:24; '. . . will know that I am He' (8:28); 'before Abraham ever was, I am' (8:58).

THE WORD AS AN ACTIVE AND CREATIVE FORCE

In the creation narratives of the Old Testament, God's Word is clearly portrayed as something alive and active. It is the commanding force by which things come into being. God says . . . and it comes into being; by this image the narratives sought to portray the truth that God created the world and all living things.

Thereafter throughout the Old Testament, the Word of God is portrayed as the power to change things.

This belief that a deity has the power to change things by a word was not new. Throughout all cultures, no matter how primitive, no matter how sophisticated, the belief in the power of sounds or words is widespread.

In some cultures this is expressed in witch-doctors and their powers. A curse spoken against one of the tribe by its witch-doctor will be fulfilled. Without going too deeply into the reasons why this might be, what is important is the power ascribed to the 'word' at the spiritual level.

When Jesus speaks to people in the Gospel, they are either called to action, or invited to change. Yet at the same time, they were left free to do as they wished. When Jesus healed the sick, his words were often surprising: 'Your sins are forgiven . . .'.

In Jesus the Word comes to bring about the reign of happiness that in their heart of hearts everyone longs for. But again, Jesus put it in a surprising way: 'The Kingdom is within you'.

Christians believe it is by taking these words to heart that they will find true peace and happiness.

DISCUSSION TOPICS
Unit 5 Session 3

What do you think about your name?

Are you happy with it?

Or would you like to change it?

Why?

Make a list
of some of the names
that various groups
are called: e.g.
yuppies; brats; pests; etc.

What do you think
of this kind of naming?

(In pairs)

What name/s do you use
for God?
Jesus? Father? Holy Spirit?
Perhaps 'Mother'
as well as 'Father'?
Do you use the same one name?
several names? many names?

Do you think
that the name
that you have for God
says anything about
the relationship
you have with your God?

Imagine that you have a three-year-old child who has just asked you to say what God is like:
- what is your reply?

UNIT 5
SESSION 4
TRUTH

WORDS AND TRUTH
Prepare this role play in advance, to provide a starting point for this session's reflection and discussion.

Characters: Mother, and her three teenage children.
Scenario: Mother has bought a new hat. It is awful!
It clashes with the coat she wants to wear, and has such a floppy brim that when she wears it it covers her face, and all you can see is her chin.

She asks her teenage children what they think of it:
- one lies and says it's lovely;
- another hedges, saying he/she has never seen anything like it before;
- the third suddenly remembers he/she has a phone call to make.

Invite the students to turn to discuss this with their neighbour: how should one handle a situation like this?

After some time, ask for comments, and discuss the situation as a group.

TRUTH
Jesus said,
    'I was born for this, for this I came into the world:
    to bear witness to the truth;
    and all who are on the side of truth listen to my voice.'
    'Truth?' said Pilate 'What is that?' (John 18:37-8 JB)
How do we know what truth is?
Is it possible to tell the truth all the time?
What would count as truth in the hat scene?
How do we handle the truth in our lives?
Are there times when we want to hear the truth, or would we prefer to hear what we'd like to hear?

Is it possible really to know the truth of anything?
How does charity fit with truth?
What should we do when the truth seems cruel?

Note: advise the students that in the coming week they have to find a short text, prose or poetry, which is meaningful to each of them. They should bring it to the discussion (i.e. second) part of Session 5.

DISCUSSION TOPICS
Unit 5 Session 4

There is a sense in which we can
never fully develop and grow as
people unless we can face
the truth about ourselves.
How would you like to be told
about areas in your life
that need to be changed?
Would you like to be told gently?
straight? with love? not at all?
that it's nobody else's business?

It is not always easy
to say just what we think
in our relationships with one another.

What, do you think,
are the reasons for this?

Imagine that you have a friend
who you know is going to die.
Your friend's parents don't want
your friend to know.
While you're visiting your friend
in hospital, he/she says,
'I've got this feeling I'm going to die.
Do you think it's true?'
How would you cope with this?
Would you tell your friend the truth?

Telling the truth is not always easy.

What would you think
of someone who said,
'I don't care what the situation is,
I always tell the truth'?

Note: for the next discussion session, please find a short text, piece of poetry, prose, or whatever, which you find meaningful. Bring this to the next session.

UNIT 5
SESSION 5
WORDS EXPRESS RELATIONSHIPS

For the input for this session, select a panel of people who will be prepared to share with the students times when words have made a difference to their lives. The panel could be made up of students/parents/group leaders/staff.

Each member of the panel is asked to share an example of something that was said to them which affirmed them, which helped their personal confidence.

It does not matter how brief the example is. What is important is that they each say in their own way how they were affected by what was said.

When the panel have presented their experiences, explore how words express the relationships that we have
- with ourselves;
- with others;
- with God.

OURSELVES

Have the students explore the words they use about themselves, e.g. have the students work in twos, where they describe themselves to each other in a few sentences.

After allowing enough time for this, reintroduce general discussion:

How many of you really told the truth?

Did you make a joke of yourself and put yourself down?

Did you say things like 'I'm OK at most things'?

How many of you were comfortable enough to say things like 'I'm a good person (most of the time)'; 'I like myself'; 'I'm good at . . .'.

How do you talk to yourself?

OTHERS

Reflect on the language you use with or towards others:

How do you speak to other people?

Does it vary according to what you think of them?

e.g. Do you speak down to some people,

but take care to speak respectfully to others?

Does what you say to people build them up or put them down?

GOD

Reflect on the language you use with or towards God:

What, if any, kind of language do you use to speak to God?

Do you use your own words? In modern English or King James English?

Do you always resort to saying set prayers? Or just sometimes?

Reflect on what it means to use set texts:

Do we do this out of 'respect' for God?

Would we do this when talking to someone in ordinary life?

With someone we considered important?

So what does it mean?

What are we really trying to say?

Note: remind the students they should have chosen a text as being meaningful to them, to bring to the group work part of this session.

DISCUSSION TOPICS
Unit 5 Session 5

'Words! Words! Words!
... I'm so sick of words!'
This is Eliza Doolittle's complaint
to Freddy in My Fair Lady.

What do we mean when we say
words are empty?

Can you think of examples of words
being spoken and not meant?

Some people resist and resent
being given set texts for prayers.

What might be their reasons for this?

Do you think they are right?
Always? Sometimes?

You were asked to bring to this discussion session
a text which was meaningful to you.
Take it in turns to present your text to the rest of your group:
read it out to them,
and explain why it is that you find it meaningful.

From SEARCH FOR MEANING, published by Geoffrey Chapman, © Judith Russi SSMN 1990.
Multiple copies may be made only by the institution which has purchased a master set.

'Truth cannot be adequately
expressed in words;
we should abandon the pretence
that we can.'

'The pen is mightier than the sword.'

'The deepest wounds
that can be inflicted on a person
are those caused by words.'

UNIT 6
SESSION 1
THE NEED TO COMMUNICATE

The aim of this session is to explore some facets of human communication:

- the deep-seated need to communicate;
- ways in which that need can be perceived;
- ways in which we attempt to communicate.

Most of us, being able-bodied, able to speak, to hear, and to see, probably take our communication skills for granted. It is when confronted with people who, despite lacking these physical means, still manage to communicate, that we begin to have some inkling of how deep within us is the need to communicate.

Use material about Helen Keller;
- or from *Under the Eye of the Clock* by Christopher Nolan (Weidenfeld and Nicolson/Pan);
- or from *My Left Foot* by Christy Brown (Palace video)

WHY DO WE COMMUNICATE?

By our very nature, we need to be in communication with the world around us. We depend for our physical survival on interchanging a whole host of signals; beyond that, to function as persons, we need to communicate with other fellow human beings.

Understanding more of this personal need to communicate is one very important key to understanding prayer.

HOW DO WE COMMUNICATE?

Have prepared pictures of the following, and hold them up for the students to see:

- pictures of different types of car, including an expensive sports car;
- pictures of youngsters distinctively dressed according to current trends (and perhaps some 'historic' ones, e.g. mods and rockers);

- a picture of a single red rose;
- picture of either an engagement or a wedding ring.

Invite the students to discuss what message or signal is being given by the people who have these things, who wear these clothes, who offer the flower or the ring.

e.g. What am I saying to the world about myself if I dress this way?

What am I trying to express when I offer an engagement ring?

These are four ways in which we try to communicate, try to express who we want people to think we are, what we feel about other people.

Often words are inadequate to express what we really feel towards another person, and we use signs and symbols.

In effect, we are trying to establish, deepen and strengthen our relationship; to come to know, and to be known by, the other person. In our quest to achieve this we augment what we can say verbally by
- body language;
- using signs and symbols.

NON-VERBAL COMMUNICATION

Have this role play prepared in advance. It is very important that no words must be uttered throughout this scene. This works best (i.e. there is better appreciation of the impact of non-verbal communication) for the group if the roles are not taken by students, but by group leaders/members of staff.

Characters: a young married couple.
Scenario: evening. At first the husband is alone. He sets/has set a beautiful table for two: flowers, candles, etc.

He keeps looking at his watch: the wife is late. Husband keeps looking in the oven. Becomes more and more agitated.

At sound of a car arriving, husband becomes calmer, and more purposeful. Looks in mirror and tidies hair. Puts a gift-wrapped package at one of the places at the table.

Wife flops in, clearly very tired. Drops briefcase, throws off coat, without caring where they land. Shuffles across to table, gets out newspaper, pushes flowers aside to make room to read it.

Husband is now clearly upset, but controlled. He gathers and tidies up the coat and briefcase. Then goes out.

After a while the wife goes to get something to eat. Discovers elaborate meal for two in the oven. Starts to look round, and gradually notices the things she missed before: the candles, the flowers, eventually the present. She reacts. At last, she has realized . . .

Encourage the students to discuss the role play, e.g.

What do we know about the husband?

That he cared; the amount of preparation is a sign of the importance he attributes to the occasion, which in turn is a sign of how he feels about his wife.

If someone is precious to us, then the means we use to convey and communicate that become precious to us.

Eventually, the gifts themselves are less important than the message we are trying to get across: this is so universally recognized that it has become a cliché: 'It's the thought that counts'.

COMMUNICATION - WITH SELF

We spend our whole life journeying into maturity. As we move along we struggle to come to terms with what life is about, we want to know what things mean. We are constantly challenged to think, evaluate, search, reflect, and even to question all we have ever learnt. The more we discover about life, the more we discover how much more there is to discover!

As we journey and so grow, we need time to reflect on where we've been, on the direction we might prefer in future. For this, we experience the need of calm, the space and peace to think things through. We feel the need to be alone, to be still, to be silent.

It can be in moments like this that the deepest communication may take place, that the deepest and truest prayers are uttered.

DISCUSSION TOPICS
Unit 6 Session 1a

Tick the column you think most appropriate
for each of these statements:

	RARELY	SOMETIMES	OFTEN	ALWAYS
When I speak to a person I look at them . . .				
When people speak to me, I make eye contact with them . . .				
During conversation I listen until the person has finished and think before I reply . . .				
Time drags when I have to listen, and don't have the chance to say much . . .				
Sometimes, in conversation, I touch the other person . . .				
I find other people's opinions fascinating . . .				
If I'm bored by the conversation I change the subject . . .				
I think I express myself clearly, and people know what I'm saying . . .				
You must always be totally honest in conversation . . .				
I don't mind talking about feelings as well as thoughts . . .				
I think body language says a lot . . .				
I avoid talking about really personal things . . .				

Share and discuss your answers with a friend.

From SEARCH FOR MEANING, published by Geoffrey Chapman, © Judith Russi SSMN 1990.
Multiple copies may be made only by the institution which has purchased a master set.

DISCUSSION TOPICS
Unit 6 Session 1b

Discuss your reactions to the wordless role play.

Have you ever used a gift to show affection?

To say sorry?

Discuss the circumstances of using a gift to say something, e.g.:

was your gift accepted?
how did you feel?

did giving the gift make it easier to talk about how you really felt?

Is there someone in your life that you can turn to as a friend, no matter what, no matter when, regardless of the problem?

What is it about them that makes you trust them?

In what circumstances, if any, would you freely choose to pray?

MY GOD!

OH GOD, NO!

People who say they don't pray will quite often utter statements like:
'Thank God for that!'
Why do you think this is?
Could these statements be prayers?

UNIT 6
SESSION 2
CONVERSATION AND PRAYER

CONVERSATION

If possible prepare the room in advance so that the group will be sitting in a semicircle. Provide some kind of focal point, e.g. a low table, with a bowl of flowers on it and a single candle. A little incense may help create a 'different' atmosphere.

However, be careful. The object is certainly not to make the group feel they are being made to pray. Explain that the room has been arranged in this way to improve the chances that:

- everyone present will feel part of the group (hence no one sitting behind anyone else);
- everyone present has the chance to listen to everyone else;
- that the candle or flowers are offered as a possible focus, to help everyone present centre their attention.

In summary, the aim is to make circumstances conducive to encouraging thoughtful, calm conversation.

We all think we know what 'conversation' is, but it may happen less than we think. For genuine conversation, the participants need to be listening to each other, as well as speaking. Perhaps the students have had the frustrating experience of trying to talk to someone who is not really listening to them.

Invite the students to wonder whether there might not have been times when they have done this to others. Our attention has been elsewhere; we'd far prefer to be left alone. Sometimes we are glad enough of the person's company, but want them to listen to us - and we have little or no time in return for what they want to say to us.

So conversation is a two-way process. It make demands on us:

- honesty;
- availability;
- empathy;
- the openness and ability to listen.

Sharing in someone else's life in this way is time-consuming. We won't always have answers for questions that may be asked of us; nor will those who listen to us always have answers for us. What matters is that our friend is with us, listening to and supporting us.

LISTEN AND REFLECT

First, make sure everyone has a pen/pencil and paper on which to jot down thoughts or reactions, as they feel appropriate.

Allow a few moments of silence. Play some quiet music to create a sense of calm, of stillness, an atmosphere of listening.

1st reading

'When you discover that someone accepts you,
you want to give everything in return,
and you discover that you have much more to give
than you thought . . .
Here is my song for the asking.
Ask me and I will play
so sweetly I'll make you smile.
This is my tune for the taking.
Take it, don't turn away.
I've been waiting all my life.
Ask me and I will play
all the love that I hold inside.'[1]

Allow a pause and invite the group to note down their reactions to this reading.

2nd reading

'Don't walk in front of me;
I may not follow.
Don't walk behind me;
I may not lead.
Walk beside me
and just be my friend.'[2]

Allow a pause and invite the group to note down their reactions to this reading.

1 .'Song for the asking': words and music by Paul Simon © 1970 Paul Simon. Recorded on the album *Bridge over troubled water* ®1970 CBS Inc.
2. Albert Camus.

3rd reading

'One night a man had a dream. He dreamed he was walking along a beach with the Lord. Across the sky flashed scenes from his life. For most scenes, there were two clear sets of footprints in the sand.

But the man noticed that for some moments in his life, there was only one set of footprints; he also noticed that this was at the lowest and saddest moments of his life.

Puzzled by this he said to the Lord,

"Lord, you promised that if I followed you, you would walk with me all the way. But look at the footprints! When things were worst for me, there's only one set! Why did you leave me when I needed you most?"

The Lord replied,

"Look more carefully. There is only one set of prints because those are the moments when I carried you."'[3]

Allow a pause and invite the group to note down their reactions to this reading.

3. *Footprints*, author unknown.

PRAYER AND PRAYING

Without forcing the point, perhaps some of the group will appreciate the parallels between conversation and prayer, between communicating with each other and communicating with God.

No two people relate to each other in exactly the same way. Because of the uniqueness of each human being, relationships on a human level are also unique. So too, relationships with God. One important consequence is that we should not attempt to force such a relationship to conform to one particular conversation (prayer) style.

'Prayer' is the technical term which we use to mean the way we relate to our God.

Over the centuries there have been innumerable ways in which people have prayed; there have been many methods of teaching people to pray. Just as guidelines may help us to develop our skills in social dialogue, so too in our prayer dialogue. But these are only guides, suggestions, pointers. Once a relationship has begun, it has a logic of its own, nothing can limit it.

Often, it is simply getting started that causes us problems, both in social conversation and in prayer. We should not shy away from help; nor should we confuse these helps with conversation or prayer itself.

Just as we use signs, symbols, gestures, actions and rituals to help express our innermost feelings in social dialogue, so too these same 'props' assist and support us in prayer.

Discuss your reactions to the readings used in the earlier part of this session:
- which, if any, of the readings did you like most?
- which reading did you like least?
- why did you react to these readings in these ways?

The readings talk about the need people have to know there is someone who will stand by them through thick and thin:
- do you think that everyone feels this need?
- do you feel this need?

In the past few years your relationships with other people have matured considerably. This is all expressed in the way you speak, your expectations of people, your expectations of yourself.

But has the way you pray been maturing?
Has it changed in any way?
Are you still reciting set texts?
Do you pay attention to and understand what you say in prayer?
Do you feel that your prayer has changed and grown with you?

Compared with, say, two years ago,
do you pray MORE/LESS/ABOUT THE SAME/NEVER?

Give reasons for your answer.

Why do you think the wearing of religious symbols, like crosses, is so popular?

Do crosses and medals mean anything to you?

UNIT 6
SESSION 3
PRAYERS OR PRAYING?

This session, perhaps more than any other, needs to be sensitive to where the students are. You need to gauge carefully, whichever avenue the students have opted for, whether it is appropriate for the session to end in prayer. If the group show a willingness to have a prayer session, the group leader should also be willing to take part. If the group decide that such a session of prayer is inappropriate, encourage them to explore objectively the phenomenon of prayer:

- why do people feel the need to pray?
- what, do the group think, are people doing when they pray?
- and for those who don't pray, what other activity fulfils the same need?
- do people get outside themselves? If so, how?

Towards the end of the last session, we were discovering the value, or perhaps even the necessity, of 'props' in conversation.

Inasmuch as prayer shares many of the features of conversation, we may need similar 'props' when we come to pray.

One such 'prop' is to use formal prayers, i.e. set, usually traditional, texts. Have the group discuss why they feel people use such formal prayers:

- it's an easier way to start, because you don't have to think what to say;
- people may feel that the person who composed the text is better at praying than they are.

The practice of formal prayers was common in Jesus' time, too. It was customary for leading rabbis (teachers) to teach their disciples formal prayers. It seems quite natural, then, to the disciples to ask Jesus,

'Lord, teach us to pray, just as John taught his disciples to pray . . .' (Luke 11:1).

The answer that Jesus offered has been taken up by Christians, and is regarded as one of the greatest Christian prayers.

However, one of the ironies is that if you look at the Gospel text closely, Jesus says he is offering a model for prayer, rather than a set text. The prayer exercise which follows attempts to pray as Jesus told us. You need to judge whether using a less well-known version (as below) will help the students; if there is a risk that this would be too distracting, or confusing, it would be better to stay with the traditional text.

The use of slides and music might help. (There are a number of commercially produced slide meditations on the Lord's Prayer; for example, that published by Franciscan Communications.)

THE LORD'S PRAYER
Our Father in heaven . . .
Staking our claim to our true parentage.
We are sons and daughters of God.
It is the Spirit within us that enables us to cry out to you,
'Abba, Father'.

. . . may your name be held holy.
Because of who you are, our Creator and source of our life.
Just as we are hurt by those who do not respect our earthly parents, so too we are hurt by those who do not recognize who you are, and your relationship with us.

Your kingdom come . . .
Your kingdom, Jesus has told us, is one where there is no
sadness or tears, where war and suffering are no more,
where death has no power;
where justice, love and peace rule.
This is the world we long for.
And to which we pledge ourselves to work.

Your will be done on earth as it is in heaven.
We believe that what you will, what you want, is the best for each of us.
What you want is for us to be truly happy.
This is what Jesus came to show us.
Is this not what we long for?

Give us each day our daily bread . . .
We look to you to be kept in life.
But we also look to you for nourishment of a deeper kind,
the kind that will give us a real life and not just an existence.
We hunger for truth and fulfilment;
too often we try and satisfy this with a diet of materialism,
selfishness and greed.

Forgive us our debts . . .
We owe so much to you:
our life; the many 'second chances' that you offer us.
We ask pardon for the continual times when we hurt others
as well as ourselves.
In sorrow we know that we are loved and forgiven.

As we forgive those who are in debt to us . . .
Lest we forget that forgiveness is a two-way process.
We ask for the strength to be as forgiving as you are;
to be forgiving from the heart, and not just in words;
to be forgiving of ourselves as well as of others.

Do not put us to the test, but save us from the evil one . . .
We do not have to live for many years before discovering
how vulnerable and weak we are.
Alone, how could we survive?
Evil is subtle and attractive;
it can be so easily disguised as good.
Grant us the wisdom to discern good from evil,
and the strength and courage to choose your way.

REFLECTIONS

When the exercise is complete, move into a gentle 'post-mortem' on it together. We have used music, slides, reflected together on the phrases of the Lord's Prayer. All of these demand or encourage a measure of emotional response:

     - is this a good thing?
     - in what ways might the emotional response be in conflict with our intellectual response?
     - is it possible to have one without the other?

ATTITUDES TOWARDS PRAYER

Elsewhere in the Gospel, Jesus offers a very clear lesson on how to pray. It is in the parable of the Pharisee and the publican (Luke 18:9-14). It might be good to explore the message of this parable through role play; the story is well enough known for the students to be able to play it out spontaneously.

Alternatively, you could divide the group into smaller groups (into twos, perhaps) and ask them to convert the parable into the world of today: instead of a Pharisee, who might Jesus have used today as an example of how not to pray? and who as an example of how to pray? Bring everyone into one group again to share their thoughts.

From Jesus' teaching it is clear that clever words, elaborate techniques or a degree in theology are no substitute for, and do not guarantee, a relationship with God. After all, they could be carried out by someone who had no belief in God. It is from a desire, from a longing to know, that we begin to discover who God is. This discovery leads to a relationship, in which we communicate with him. This is when prayer happens.

DISCUSSION TOPICS
Unit 6 Session 3

The need to communicate, to 'get in touch with'
someone greater has been a constant
throughout human history.
Do you think the help and training
you have received throughout your life
have been effective in helping you discover
who God is for you?
What are your views on formal prayers
being said in school/college/church?

In twos, work out a modern-day presentation
of the parable of the Pharisee and the publican
(Luke 18): who might Jesus have chosen
instead of a Pharisee? instead of a publican?
where would the action take place?
Show your interpretation to the rest of the group.
Share and discuss your reactions.

Is there someone you really admire?
Who is it? Why do you admire him/her?
If you could meet that person,
what would you want to say to him/her?
What would you want him/her to know about you?
How do you think you would react?
What effect do you think
such a meeting would have on you?
How do you think you would react to someone
who claimed he/she didn't admire anyone?

Exchange ideas about the role of ritual in our society.
For example, what do you think of the chanting,
singing, wearing of team colours,
carrying team mascots,
that accompanies big football matches?
What do you think of the way that 'stars'
(film, TV and music personalities, etc.)
and their way of dress are copied by fans?
Some people go to great lengths to keep
in touch with their 'hero/heroine',
writing to fan clubs, etc.
Why do you think this is?
What is it that makes people behave this way?

From SEARCH FOR MEANING, published by Geoffrey Chapman, © Judith Russi SSMN 1990.
Multiple copies may be made only by the institution which has purchased a master set.

UNIT 6
SESSION 4
WAYS OF PRAYING

This session will put before the students various ways of praying, which some people have found useful. Be careful to remain open in presenting them. They are no more than tools. There are many others, and these could be included as appropriate, or used for further development (e.g. Benedictine, Ignatian, Franciscan, the Little Way of Thérèse of Lisieux, etc.).

Before this session, have several groups of students prepare short examples of some of the various ways in which people might pray. For example, a dance to a psalm; use of short text extracts as the basis for meditation.

There are many ways of praying. All have their own worth and value. We can pray:
- alone;
- with another person;
- in a group;
- as a community.

In each of these situations prayer can be:
- silent;
- shared;
- scripture-based;
- based on poetry, prose;
- formal;
- informal;
- ritualistic;
- through dance, music, mime, drama;
- using nature;
- using art;
- using signs, symbols.

Indeed, prayer can be expressed through a combination of one or more of these.

Encourage the students to explore when they think these might help their prayer.

Should we expect our prayer to remain always the same?

Should the means we use always remain the same?

Might there be times when we don't need any of these means? e.g. just as a couple can reach a point in their relationship when words are no longer necessary, just being with each other is enough.

LIFE AS PRAYER

When we are close to someone we might say that we will do something because of our relationship with them. And we may carry out doing this something even when separated from them. That something can then become not only a reminder of the other person, but a gesture of contact beyond the separation: 'Every time I . . ., I'll be thinking of you'. What we do may be trivial in others' eyes. But when we believe in the other person's love enough, we are willing to risk what may seem stupid to someone else.

So too with those who offer their life to God as prayer. They are saying: 'Everything that I do today, I will do for you, Lord'.

PLACES FOR PRAYER

Where can we pray?

- at home;
- in your room;
- in church;
- in a chapel;
- travelling to/from work;
- as you work;
- whilst relaxing;
- going for a walk;
- in bed;
- etc.

TIME FOR PRAYER/REFLECTION

Just as the place should be chosen to fit individual need and temperament, so too the time.

But making time is essential.

DISCUSSION TOPICS
Unit 6 Session 4

I need space . . .
I just want to be . . .
The trouble with so-and-so is
they just don't know
who they are.

What do you think of these
statements?

Are you comfortable
with silence?

Are you comfortable
with being alone?

Work out the reasons
for your answers.

Time just to be still . . .
time to think . . .
time to reflect . . .
time to pray . . .

How important do you
think this is?

SNAP!

SILENCE

LIBRARY

(In small groups)

Discuss the ways that you feel
are the most conducive,
the most helpful
for reflection/prayer.

Do you use music, text,
pictures, etc.
to help you reflect?

Prepare a short reflection time,
using whatever resources you think most appropriate.

From SEARCH FOR MEANING, published by Geoffrey Chapman, © Judith Russi SSMN 1990.

UNIT 6
SESSION 5
SHARING EXPERIENCES OF PRAYER

The input for this session should be to invite four individuals to share with the group their experience of prayer. How do they pray? What does it mean to them?

Try and invite a balanced choice of four from the following:

- someone who is a member of a charismatic prayer group;
- a young person;
- someone from one of the Non-conformist Churches;
- someone from a non-Christian faith;
- an elderly person;
- someone from a religious order;
- a member of an evangelical Church.

DISCUSSION TOPICS
Unit 6 Session 5

When/if you are a parent,
do you think you would want
your children to learn to pray?
Offer your reasons.

Does your family pray together?
If so, when?

Are there types of prayer that you don't like?
Talk about these together,
saying why you don't like them.

Have you ever asked someone to pray for you
(regardless of how you feel about prayer)?

Would you like more opportunity to think/reflect/pray
about your life, and about who you are?

Do you feel you have been given the skills needed
to enable you to pray/reflect?

Try and offer reasons for your answer.

Which of these do you find most helpful:
- praying/reflecting alone?
- praying/reflecting with a friend?
- praying/reflecting in a church?
- none of these?
- do different things help at different times?

What are your reactions
to the guest speakers' views on prayer?

Which of the speakers did you find most interesting?
Did any of their ideas surprise you?
Try to offer reasons for your reactions.

'Prayer is like an insurance policy;
you do it just in case!'

'The problem with communication
is that it is impossible to be
totally honest and totally kind
at the same time.'

'Belief in the effectiveness of prayer
would be more credible
if those who pray showed some sign
of having benefited from it.'

UNIT 7

It would be as well to make sure the students understand that the sessions throughout this theme cannot offer an in-depth study of humanism, materialism, capitalism, Marxism and Communism. Our aim is to explore what kind of challenge these 20th-century secular philosophies offer to the Christian philosophy.

In each session, try and establish a brief statement of the essence of the '-isms', and a comparison with Christianity.

UNIT 7
SESSION 1
HUMANISM

'Man is the measure of all things.'
(Protagoras, 5th century BC)

Humanism is an ideology which stresses the capacity of individuals to solve their own problems, to advance the course of human knowledge, to improve their environment by ultimate reference to the human mind.

Auguste Comte (1798-1857) depicted God as **humanity**. His humanism presented love as its first principle, order as its basis, and progress as its aim.

Humanism shares some common concerns with Christianity:

inasmuch as it stresses the dignity and potential of the individual;

in the importance it accords to concern for others, and the need for compassion and charity;

in its vision of the advancement of the human spirit to its fullest potential.

Humanism interprets the 'spirit' in a person's life, not in any religious sense, but rather as the power of human determination; it goes beyond the individual, as the transfer of potential and striving from one generation to the next.

However, humanism is atheistic in nature, and preaches total faith in the individual. Religion is seen either as a prop for those who lack the courage to face the problems and mysteries of life on totally human terms, or as a camouflage for not dealing with fundamental problems. For example, prayer would be seen as uselessly petitioning God instead of acting; it is putting trust in a myth instead of a person's ability to act.

DISCUSSION TOPICS
Unit 7 Session 1

ROLE PLAY
Characters and scenario:
>   One person in the group has recently lost a close
>   relative.
>   Two friends call to console him/her,
>   one of whom is a committed Christian,
>   the other a humanist.
>
>   With due respect for the sensitivity of the situation,
>   act out what you think might happen.

Imagine that you are living in a country struck by famine.
What would your reaction be:
-   if you were a humanist?
-   if you were a Christian?
Discuss your views with your group.

Do you think human beings are capable of solving every problem
themselves?
Give examples to back up your point of view.

What do you think motivates those who do not believe in God
to be good?

How far do you think it is true to say that Jesus was 'humanist' in his
teachings?

What do you make of these statements?

Religion is a compensation for
the lack of scientific
knowledge.

Only by being fully human
can we come to know God.

How would you reply to those
who make this claim?

What do you think this means?
What do you think is the basis of
this statement?

From SEARCH FOR MEANING, published by Geoffrey Chapman, © Judith Russi SSMN 1990.
Multiple copies may be made only by the institution which has purchased a master set.

UNIT 7
SESSION 2
CAPITALISM

Capitalism is a philosophy based on the private ownership of the means of production.

The historical origins lie in the transfer of economic life from an agrarian to an urban economy in the course of the 16th, 17th and 18th centuries; but it is essentially associated with the Industrial Revolution in 19th-century Western Europe.

In political terms, it is almost exclusively linked to the liberal democracies, as exists in most Western states.

The capitalist ethic encourages an entrepreneurial spirit, self-reliance of the individual, choice for the consumer, competition to ensure choice, freedom and low prices, and the justification of the profit motive.

Christianity would share its respect for individual freedom, its encouragement of self-opportunity, and self-advancement by using gifts, talents and potential. But Christianity would oppose the massing of wealth in very few hands, exploitation of individuals or of whole sectors of society, or of developing poorer nations all for the sake of profit.

Christianity would oppose the more strident form of capitalism which results in a lack of compassion or even consideration for those unable to compete effectively, for the unemployed.

DISCUSSION TOPICS
Unit 7 Session 2

ROLE PLAY
Characters and scenario:
> *A middle-aged couple are watching the news on television.*
> *The major news stories are:*

> *'Multi-millionaire Robert Murdosh breaks all records for newspaper sales. Rival newspapers join forces with unions to protest against unfair practices.'*

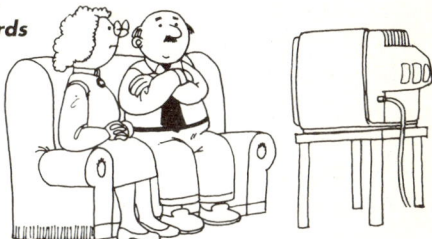

> *'Unemployment returns to three million. Record demand for Social Security benefits.'*

> *A debate/argument begins.*
> *One defends competition and free market forces;*
> *the other argues vehemently against a system which can cause such inequalities.*

Most capitalist societies claim to be Christian.
What do you think of this? Is this possible?

How far can a Christian accept the 'profit motive'?
Give reasons for your answer.

The history of the application of capitalism is of 'slump-boom' alternation. What implications are there here for human dignity? Use examples to back up your view.

Capitalist societies are class-based.
Can class-based societies be Christian in nature?
Try to back up your response by reference to examples from scripture.

Read and explore (e.g., by acting out with modern day references):
- the parable of the talents (Luke 19:11-27);
- the parable of the workers in the vineyard (Matthew 20:1-16).

Compare what these parables put forward with the tenets of capitalism. Share your findings with your group.

From SEARCH FOR MEANING, published by Geoffrey Chapman, © Judith Russi SSMN 1990.
Multiple copies may be made only by the institution which has purchased a master set.

UNIT 7
SESSION 3
MATERIALISM

A 19th-century philosophy, materialism states that nothing exists except tangible reality. In other words, acknowledging the existence only of the material world, and denying the spiritual world.

In our time, materialism has come to mean the pursuit and accumulation of material wealth as the driving purpose of existence.

Wealth is the main or ultimate aim in life. Materialism is atheistic in nature, maintaining that since there is existence only for human beings, the main motive should be to make that existence as comfortable and pleasurable as possible.

One point where materialism and Christianity might agree is in accepting the need for all to live in due dignity, and sharing the fruits of the earth.

Christianity would oppose the greed and selfishness that materialism induces. This runs directly counter to the very heart of Christianity's unselfish love, and the precept to share material wealth with those who have less.

Christianity would also take issue with the way materialism judges an individual's worth or success by the amount and quality of his/her possessions.

DISCUSSION TOPICS
Unit 7 Session 3a

What do you think gives a person status in today's society?
List five examples:

Discuss your selection with a friend.
Does your list contain more material things, or more human qualities?

Think of two people who are world famous, but have contrasting lifestyles:
one rich, with many material possessions;
the other who uses only what is needed for day to day living.

Discuss your examples.
Say how you feel about the way each lives out his/her Christian life.

> There is no world beyond the one we can see, hear and feel.

> Greed and power are the main motivating forces in today's world.

Discuss each of these statements:
do you agree with them? disagree? wholly? partly?

Offer examples and reasons to back up your opinions.

From SEARCH FOR MEANING, published by Geoffrey Chapman, © Judith Russi SSMN 1990.
Multiple copies may be made only by the institution which has purchased a master set.

DISCUSSION TOPICS
Unit 7 Session 3b

Money is the root of all evil.

If you want to be perfect, go sell all you have and give it to the poor. Then come, follow me.

How would you respond to this proverb?
And what do you make of what Jesus said
to the rich young man?
Discuss your reactions.

Choose a magazine or newspaper and, in small groups, have a critical look at the adverts.
Pick one advert, and ask what is the real message (behind the words like 'essential', 'exclusive') that is being conveyed.
What is that these adverts are encouraging people to do or to be?

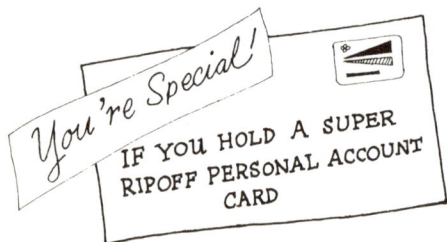

You're Special!

IF YOU HOLD A SUPER RIPOFF PERSONAL ACCOUNT CARD

Compare and contrast the two people caricatured here.
How far do you judge a person by what they possess?
Discuss this in your groups.

UNIT 7
SESSION 4
MARXISM

Marxism takes its name from, and is based on the teachings of, Karl Marx. The son of a rabbi, Karl Marx was born in Trier, Germany in 1818. He studied law and economics at Berlin University. While at Berlin, he became interested in the writings of the German philosopher Friedrich Hegel.

Hegel had developed a philosophy known as 'dialectics': this was based on perceiving the essential development of understanding as arising from the conflict of ideas. Marx adapted this to take account of what he believed to be a scientific approach to the progress of human history; this Marx called 'dialectical materialism'.

Marx believed that at each stage of human history human beings stood in opposition to each other in class conflict. This conflict was related to ownership of the means of production in any society: those who owned such means versus those who did not.

In ancient times, this conflict was between the slaves and the free classes; in medieval times, it was between those who owned land and those who did not, but were forced to work the land; in Marx's time, in the industrial capitalist society, the conflict was between the owners of the business and the capital ('the bourgeoisie'), and those who were forced to work for wages ('the proletariat').

Marx argued that if only the proletariat, who were in the majority, would realize the power they had, they could overthrow the bourgeoisie in a socialist revolution and could distribute the wealth of society fairly among the workers. Once this redistribution of wealth was complete, history would enter its ultimate phase, 'communism'.

Marx was expelled from Germany because his writings were judged subversive. He moved to Belgium and France, and, expelled from these two, finally found a home in London.

Two major books by Marx:

The Communist Manifesto (1848), written with his friend Friedrich Engels, in which they develop the theories of history and the inevitability of class conflict;

Das Kapital (1867), which is an examination of the capitalist system. A key theme is that of 'surplus value', whereby Marx showed that in capitalist societies there was an inevitable tendency towards conflict because the employers were seeking maximum return on their investment and capital; whereas the workers' wages had to come from the surplus value at which the goods were sold. Another key theme is that of 'alienation'.

Marx died in 1883, and is buried in Highgate cemetery. His ideas are the main influence and basis of modern Communist societies.

DISCUSSION TOPICS
Unit 7 Session 4

Discuss:

Marxism highlights the huge
inequalities in society,
and points to the
inevitability of revolution
as the only solution.

What are your views on this?

What does Christianity say
about the unfair
distribution of wealth?
Do both Christianity and
Marxism condemn the vast
inequalities of
wealth in our society?
What solution does
Christianity offer?

Marxism believes
that it is possible to achieve
perfection on earth.

Does Christianity?

Some people argue
that Marxism preaches
violent revolution;
that Christianity is
essentially non-violent.

Would you agree?
Do you think violence can
ever be justified?

UNIT 7
SESSION 5
COMMUNISM

Two thirds of the world's population today live under Communist systems of government, and it has been the fastest growing ideology of the 20th century.

Its theoretical base lies in the thinking of Karl Marx: i.e. a scientific principle of history in which class conflict would lead to the eradication of a dominant class, leaving a classless society within which wealth would be distributed

'from each according to his ability,
to each according to his need'.

The first successful Marxist-inspired revolution took place in Russia in 1917. This led to the establishment of a dictatorship of the Communist Party. After World War II, Communist influence spread throughout Eastern Europe; by 1949 Soviet-style governments had been imposed in all countries 'liberated' by the Russians; in 1989-90 most of these changed considerably.

Also in 1949, China, containing something like one third of the world's population, became a Communist state. Subsequently Communist governments have taken root in other parts of Asia (North Korea, Vietnam, Laos, Kampuchea), Latin America (Cuba), and Africa.

Most Western countries have active Communist parties, most prominently in France and Italy. These parties are independent of Moscow, and develop what they term 'Euro-Communism'.

Christianity would accept the need for fairer redistribution of wealth, and the concern for the common good. Indeed, the description of the early Church by Luke in Acts 2 represents a basic, primitive communism. Christianity would also share the concept of a worldwide family, and the removal of class and race divisions.

Christianity opposes the intolerance of Communism, the manipulation of the individual, the exploitation of class divisions and hatreds, and attempts to impose the Communist ideology.

In its original Marxist sense, Communism is essentially atheistic. Marx called religion the 'opiate of the people': that it drugged the proletariat's sensibilities to their oppression by preaching acceptance and humility in this world, with the promise of reward in the next. As such, religion was a tool of exploitation and alienation.

DISCUSSION TOPICS
Unit 7 Session 5a

Dom Helder Câmara is the retired Archbishop of Recifé in Brazil: a country with one of the fastest growing economies in the world; yet the majority of its people live in poverty. He said:

'When I give food to the poor,
they call me a saint.
When I ask why the
poor have no food,
they call me a
Communist.'

What do you think he means?

Luke gives us this description of the early Church (Acts 2):
'The faithful all lived together and owned everything in common; they sold their goods and possessions and shared out the proceeds among themselves according to what each one needed.
They went as a body to the Temple every day, but met in their houses for the breaking of bread; they shared their food gladly and generously; they praised God and were looked up to by everyone.'

How does this compare with Communism? Develop your answer as much as possible, finding similarities and contrasts.

Yuri Below spent a total of 15 years in prisons, labour camps and psychiatric hospitals, before being allowed to leave the USSR in 1979. He attributes his own freedom to Western publicity for his case.
'I personally consider it especially important in helping prisoners and persecuted believers in the USSR to give prompt publicity to all cases of persecution known to us and not to forget about these people but to remind the world again and again of their fate as it unfolds. It is also most important to take every opportunity to remind Soviet representatives in the West - diplomats, journalists, trade officials and participants in every kind of delegation - of the fate of believers, and to demand their release from prison, an end to repressions directed against them and permission to emigrate for those who do not want or are unable to remain any longer in an atheist society. My greatest wish is that this list should not remain simply a record on paper but may spearhead international solidarity with the victims of state atheism in the USSR.'

What does this extract indicate about religious freedom in Communist society?

DISCUSSION TOPICS
Unit 7 Session 5b

Do you think there is
more in common:
- between Communism
  and Christianity?
- or between capitalism
  and Christianity?

Discuss your views
with the group.

To what extent, do you think,
is it true to say that
religion is a middle-class
phenomenon in modern day
Britain?

To what extent has
Communism succeeded
in appealing to the poor
because religion
has failed them?

Support your response
with examples.

Can Communism be said
to be a religion, in that:
- it has a doctrine;
- which explains
  human existence;
- and seeks a
  worldwide audience?

'Religion is the opiate of the people.'

'Religion is no longer
the principal system
of belief in Great Britain,
and therefore should not be imposed
in schools.'

'The main problem in society today
is that it can't tell need from greed.'

UNIT 8
SESSION 1
THE GREAT SCANDAL - DIVIDED CHRISTIANITY

Christians believe in one God, Father, Son and Holy Spirit; three persons in perfect unity and love.

The Church has been given the task of continuing Jesus' work of proclaiming the Good News to the world; and, like Jesus, being the sign of the love and unity of God. In the last few hours before his arrest and crucifixion, Jesus prayed for that unity:

'May they all be one.
Father, may they be one in us,
as you are in me and I am in you . . .
May they be so completely one
that the world will realize
that it was you who sent me . . .'
(John 17:21ff.).

The Church is called to witness to the Gospel in the midst of sin and division; called to serve the poor, the marginalized, those who are insignificant in the eyes of society; called to be present at every level of life on earth (politics, science, industry, etc.); called to heal the divisions between rich and poor, powerful and powerless.

But how can the Church be a credible sign of the kingdom of God and its values, how can it challenge a divided world, when it itself is equally divided?

Use the chart (Worksheet 8:1a) to explore the historical developments of divisions in the Church, and the principal doctrinal differences.

Only a Church which is itself a sign of unity and reconciliation will be able to challenge effectively the inequalities in our society today, whether those inequalities are religious, social, racial or economic.

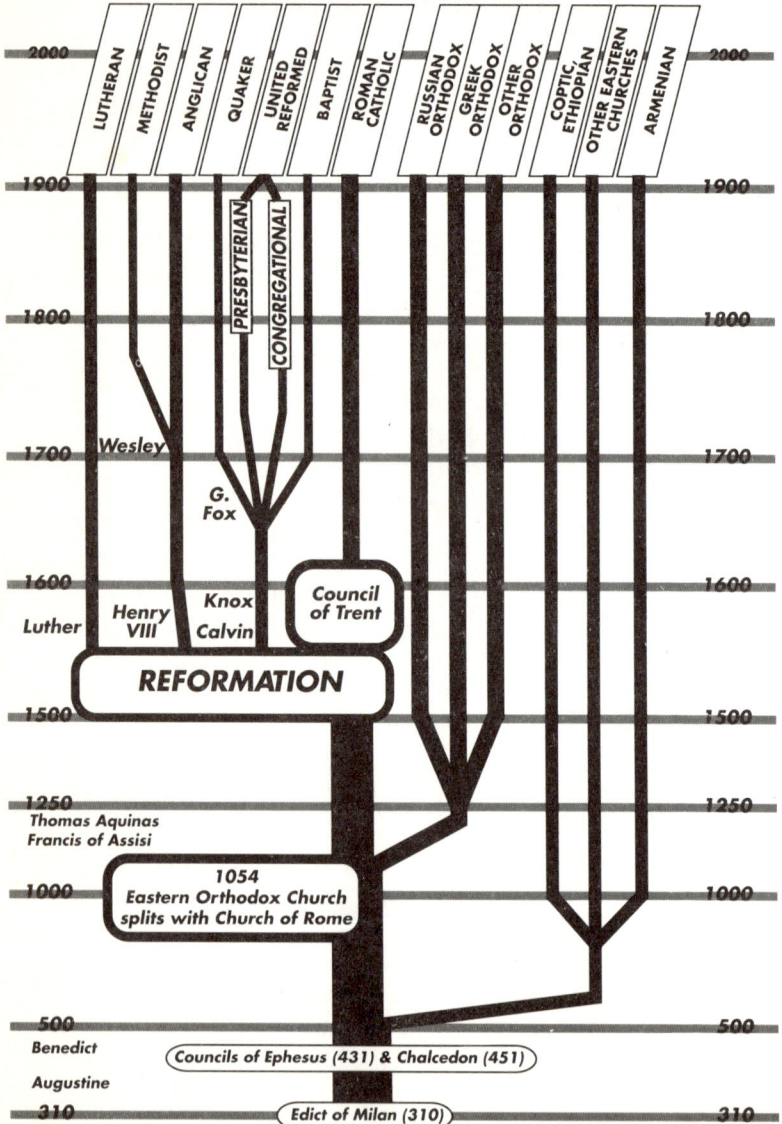

Timeline scale (left and right): 2000, 1900, 1800, 1700, 1600, 1500, 1250, 1000, 500, 310

Column headings (denominations): LUTHERAN, METHODIST, ANGLICAN, QUAKER, UNITED REFORMED, BAPTIST, ROMAN CATHOLIC, RUSSIAN ORTHODOX, GREEK ORTHODOX, OTHER ORTHODOX, COPTIC, ETHIOPIAN, OTHER EASTERN CHURCHES, ARMENIAN

PRESBYTERIAN

CONGREGATIONAL

Wesley

G. Fox

Knox

Luther

Henry VIII

Calvin

Council of Trent

REFORMATION

Thomas Aquinas
Francis of Assisi

1054
Eastern Orthodox Church
splits with Church of Rome

Benedict

Augustine

Councils of Ephesus (431) & Chalcedon (451)

Edict of Milan (310)

How many different Christian Churches are represented in your group?

Examine the chart (8:1a) tracing the divisions in the Christian Church:
how many of the different Christian Churches were you aware of?

What do you think about the divisions in the Christian Church?

In your own experience of a Christian Church, would you say that its members were open and welcoming towards members of other Christian Churches?

What is your impression of the attitudes of Roman Catholics that you know towards other Christian Churches?

'The message of the Gospel cannot be fully effective until it is proclaimed by a more united Christian Church.'

Would you agree?

UNIT 8
SESSION 2
PILGRIMS

In the first session we traced, however generally, how we come to have so many different Christian Churches throughout the world. In this present session we focus more on the British experience of ecumenical initiatives.

BACKGROUND HISTORY

The history of ecumenism is one of journey from competition to co-operation to commitment.

Pilgrimages feature prominently in all of the great religious traditions. Christianity is no exception. The early pilgrimages were to Jerusalem and the Holy Land. By the Middle Ages pilgrimages to important religious centres were very common. These were Rome, Jerusalem, Canterbury (cf. Chaucer's *Canterbury Tales*), Santiago de Compostela. This last was especially influential, and clear traces of it remain to this day. As we do today, pilgrims liked to take home some souvenir, tangible evidence that they had completed their journey. Since the majority of the pilgrims were poor, the pilgrims to Compostela simply picked up scallop shells. This soon came to be the traditional symbol by which pilgrims (first those to Compostela, later all pilgrims) came to be recognized, almost like a passport.

The ecumenical movement in Britain is now on pilgrimage, not now of individuals and small groups, but of Churches in search of reconciliation and understanding.

1910

Missionaries from many different countries met in Edinburgh to discuss evangelization in the world. They soon came to see that their efforts lacked credibility because of their internal squabbles and divisions. In fact, most missionary effort was consumed in trying to outdo each other in the acquisition of new members and converts (not excluding 'poaching' members from each other!).

One positive outcome of this meeting was a change in

attitude: the Churches tried to rid themselves of this competi-
tiveness, and looked instead to ways in which they could co-
operate.

1942
The British Council of Churches was formed. Its members were
the Anglican Church, and the other Reformed Churches.

1948
The World Council of Churches was formed. This included the
Eastern Orthodox Churches.

1964
The Second Vatican Council officially committed itself to work
for Christian unity.

1972
Establishment of the United Reformed Church, comprising the
Congregationalist and Presbyterian Churches. The Churches
of Christ joined in 1981.

In Wales, the Anglican, Methodist, Presbyterian, United
Reformed and some Baptist Churches covenanted for unity.

NOT STRANGERS, BUT PILGRIMS
This important ecumenical initiative began in 1985, when 36
Churches from mainland Britain (the Irish Churches sent
observers) met to search for ways in which together they
might start to build real unity.

Not long before, on his Glasgow visit Pope John Paul II said,
'We are only pilgrims on this earth, making our way towards
that heavenly kingdom promised to us as God's children. For
the future, can we not make that pilgrimage together hand in
hand?'

We are witnessing a much greater convergence of understanding among the Churches about the Christian faith. There
is a very high level of international theological dialogue. Very
little is now done in any of the mainstream Churches without
an eye to the ecumenical implications: for example, the debate
within the Anglican Church about the ordination of women

explicitly takes into account the tradition and attitudes of the Roman Catholic and the Orthodox Churches.

There have also been improvements in the relationships between the 'older' Churches and the 'younger' Churches, especially, for example, the black-led Churches in inner-city areas.

Most valuably, there have been over 500 local ecumenical projects: local churches have committed themselves to work for special projects that were experiments in working together, so as to give more effective witness to the Gospel.

One of the most obvious consequences of the meeting of the 36 Christian Churches was the Lent 1986 joint project. This was a programme entitled 'What on earth is the Church for?': over a million people took part in this course, in something like 65,000 house groups. 57 local radio stations were involved in broadcasting the input material for the course, which was also available on cassette.

The feedback from this first programme led to four conferences. The final one was for representatives of all mainland British Churches, who met together at Swanwick (Derbyshire). It was this conference that led the Churches to the most historic part of their pilgrimage so far: it was the move from co-operation to commitment.

This was a commitment to continue to work and pray together; but further than that, they committed themselves to finding ways in which the Churches really could unite together as a more effective symbol of the one Kingdom which Christ entrusted them to build.

THE FUTURE

Consultations have been going on to establish what form this commitment will take. In 1989, the fruits of this consultation were presented in the form of final proposals to the Churches.

1990 was the target date for the implementation of the proposals.

What is your reaction to the various efforts being made at an official level towards Christian unity? Would you:
- agree that it is good news, and should be encouraged?
- not be too happy about it?
- think it was not a good idea?
- not be bothered?

Offer reasons for your attitude.

The official representatives and Church leaders may be trying to unite the Churches. But what is the mood amongst the people in the pews? How easy or difficult do you think it will be to convince the people of the value of unity?

The Swanwick Conference looked at the area of liturgy and worship. Do you think:
- we should keep our own liturgy?
- we should scrap all denominational worship and work together to find ways in which all Christians can worship and pray together?
- we should keep our traditional ways of celebrating liturgy, but should also develop new methods of united worship which can be open to all Christians?

Prepare a short liturgical celebration that you feel would be suitable for all Christian denominations, and so could be used in any Church.

UNIT 8
SESSION 3
NO LONGER STRANGERS -
BUT PILGRIMS!

As input for this session, invite two representatives from other Christian Churches to come and talk about their own Church, and how they feel about ecumenism.

Here are some key themes that they ought to cover:

- what Christian Church do they belong to? They should describe its principal features.

- how did they come to be a member of that Church? at what age? why?

- in their opinion, how does being a member of their Church differ from being a member of any other Christian Church?

- what are their feelings about the ecumenical movement? in principle? at national or 'official' level? at local level?

- how would they like to see the Christian Churches in the future? any concrete or practical suggestions for co-operation at local level?

- do they think a united Christian Church will ever happen?

DISCUSSION TOPICS
Unit 8 Session 3

In your groups,
share and discuss your
reactions to the guest
speakers.

Do you think
Christian unity
will come about
in our lifetime?

Give reasons
for your answer.

ROLE PLAY

Characters: Three representatives of Churches, one TV interviewer.
Scenario: The 'representatives' should pick one of the Christian Churches
             about which they are suitably well informed; they will then
             speak on behalf of that Church.
             The fourth person has to act as the interviewer for a
             programme on 'Divided Christianity'.
             The topic for discussion can be:
             - either 'the role of women in the Church';
             - or 'authority in the Church'.
In the discussion, try to represent the views of the Churches fairly, as well
as giving voice to individual opinions.
What were the conclusions, if any? Were you able to reach any agreement?
If so, what was it? If not, why not? How much do you think the real life
situation was reflected in your role play?

How do you feel
personally about the
Christian Churches uniting?

Do you think
it will be possible
without major changes
within the Churches?

Cardinal Hume has made
a strong commitment
to working for unity.

To what extent, do you think,
is he supported
by the clergy?
by the lay people?

UNIT 8
SESSION 4
ECUMENISM AND
DENOMINATIONAL SCHOOLS

ENGLAND AND WALES

Balfour Act 1902

Developed 1870 legislation which had recognized the importance of links between State and Church in education. The
Balfour Act established the dual system (central government
contributes 85 per cent of the capital cost of a Voluntary Aided
School, local authorities are responsible for the day to day
running costs of the school; the Church finances the final 15 per
cent).

Butler Act 1944

Ironed out the practical difficulties in the implementation of the
Balfour Act, and established guidelines as to how State and
Church should co-operate.

Religious education and collective worship were set as an
essential part of school life for both secular and religious
educational institutes.

By this Act, the Churches became partners in the process of
educating the nation's children. The religious traditions of
Church schools were now protected.

Catholic Education Council 1955

Stated that 'the Catholic child from the Catholic home should
continue their education at the hands of Catholic teachers in a
Catholic school'.

This attitude soon drew criticism from both within and
outside the Catholic community: it was condemned as encouraging a ghetto mentality, which disregarded the outside world.
Anglican schools were subject to broadly the same criticism for
being too inward looking and exclusive.

174

Gaudium et Spes 1965 (Vatican II)

The Vatican Council urged the Church to turn outwards, to go out to the world, and take up the challenge of facing and shaping contemporary society. This was to have far-reaching implications on the aims of Catholic schools.

Signposts and homecomings

In 1981 a report from influential Catholic educationalists was submitted to the Bishops of England and Wales. This called for a 'reappraisal of the model of Church; not an institution defending a closed educational system, but a servant to the community "involved in the general task of education for its own sake"'. Not that Catholic schools ought simply to be assimilated into surrounding secular society. Church schools retain a prophetic role, 'making a distinctive and critical contribution'. Confidence to move outwards is based on the supportive community of faith where 'initiation is into a living and growing tradition, not a static body of catechetical knowledge'.

Living and sharing our faith

In the 1980s, the Catholic Bishops' Conference of England and Wales set up a National Project of Catechesis and Religious Education to aid the growth and development of the faith of Catholics at different ages, situations and stages in their faith journey. In 1988 the National Project produced the document *Our Schools and our Future - a pastoral concern and challenge.*

It is in the work of the National Project that the Catholic Church of England and Wales has been re-examining basic and fundamental questions:

Why are we paying out such vast sums of money on Catholic schools?

Are they different from state schools?

If they are different, how are they different?

What is the aim of the Catholic school?

Is denominational schooling the right way to educate our children today?

Religious Dimension of Education in a Catholic school (Rome, 1988)

'The Catholic school finds its true justification in the mission of the Church; it is based on an educational philosophy in which faith, culture and life are brought into harmony. Through it, the local Church evangelizes, educates, and contributes to the formation of a healthy and morally sound life-style among its members. The Holy Father affirms that "the need for the Catholic school becomes evidently clear when we consider what it contributes to the development of the mission of the People of God, to the dialogue between Church and the human community, to the safeguarding of the freedom of conscience". Above all, according to the Holy Father, the Catholic school helps in achieving a double objective: "of its nature it guides men and women to human and Christian perfection, and at the same time helps them to become mature in their faith. For those who believe in Christ, these are two facets of a single reality".'

Other faiths?

The Churches in the Voluntary Aided system enjoy a privileged position that other faiths do not have. Sikhs and Muslims have been actively campaigning for equivalent status for their children and schools. The Swann Report of 1985 did not recommend this.

The key question today is to discuss whether denominational schooling helps or hinders the cause of ecumenism.

DISCUSSION TOPICS
Unit 8 Session 4

In your groups, share your experiences of the schools you have attended.
Have they all been Church schools?

Would you say that
denominational schools are:
- essential for bringing children
up in their faith?
- a help, but not essential?
- on the whole more caring than
non-denominational schools?
- divisive and should be replaced
by Christian schools?
Discuss in your groups.

How much did you learn
about other Christian
denominations in your school?

In what way, if at all, was
your school involved in the
movement for Christian unity?

Was it taken seriously?
by staff? by students?

Arrange an exchange between your own group, and one 'parallel' to it, e.g.
- one being Roman Catholic,
- the other Church of England/Episcopalian, or Church of Scotland.
Each group should try and discern in what ways the 'ethos' of their groups
is the same or different.
For example:
- how much time is given to religious education?
- are there times for prayer and worship?
- if you are a school or college group, do you have a chaplain?
and if so, what is the chaplain's role?

UNIT 8
SESSION 5
MISSION AND SERVICE TOGETHER

Christians are charged with the challenge of bringing the Gospel to the whole world. The challenge is not just to proclaim the Good News in words, but in action: to **be** the Good News. Christians are called to a complete response: word-life-action.

Of its very nature, Christianity is also missionary. We are commanded by Jesus,

'Go out to the whole world . . . '

High among Christian priorities must be the building up of community, the struggle for justice and peace in the face of inequality and injustice, wherever these are to be found.

Christians are called to act justly, to love tenderly and to walk humbly with their God (cf. Micah).

Is it not time that all Christians joined together in a common evangelization, to a common witnessing to the message of Jesus Christ, in a common response to the cry of the poor?

Is it not a waste of valuable resources to be working only in our denominational camps when we could be sharing our expertise and resources to the greater benefit of all?

Use Cardinal Hume's statement to the Swanwick Conference, as appropriate.

DISCUSSION TOPICS
Unit 8 Session 5

What efforts have you seen in your own parish to encourage:
- greater understanding of other Christian Churches?
- worship sharing with the people of other Christian Churches?

Have you ever attended a united Christian service?
Why did you go?
How did you feel about it?

Are there any activities in your area that are consciously organized on an ecumenical basis?
If so, how often are they? Describe them.
If not, why do you think this might be?

What suggestions could you make to reorganize what happens in your area so that the Churches might work more together?

ROLE PLAY
Scenario:
   Imagine that a decision has been made in your area to hold a united mission for all the Christian Churches.
   Clergy will visit the homes of people from other denominations to encourage them to come to the mission.
   The mission worship services will be held in the town hall, as 'neutral ground', rather than in the building of a particular denomination.
   Divide into small groups, to role play being a family.

Characters:
   One of the household is Christian, but never goes to church;
   another is an old-fashioned committed Catholic who does not approve of mixing with 'Protestants';
   the other two aren't sure what they believe.
   They are watching the TV one evening, when the doorbell rings:
   it is the visiting clergyman, calling to speak to the family.
   He is not from the same Church as anyone in the house.

   What happens?

Read the Swanwick Declaration.
What are your reactions?

Invite some of the local clergy to visit and share their views on how the Churches might become more united. Share your views with them.

From SEARCH FOR MEANING, published by Geoffrey Chapman, © Judith Russi SSMN 1990.
Multiple copies may be made only by the institution which has purchased a master set.

'The Christian community was never united,
and is unlikely ever to be so.
The Acts of the Apostles and the Epistles
show us that one of
the key features of the early Church was
the diversity amongst the local churches.
Why destroy this rich diversity?'

'Ecumenism is bogged down
in theological debate,
which most ordinary Christians
have little time for.
While the leaders talk and debate,
the people have jumped the hurdles
and are "running the race".'

'The Christian Church
will not become
a serious voice in society
until it unites.'

CONCLUDING UNIT
DISCIPLESHIP AND MISSION
- TO WHOM ARE WE SENT?

Two differences to how things are structured for this concluding unit:

> - if the programme has been operating route reselection at the start of each unit, then ask the students to remain in the groupings they chose for the previous session. This will enable the students to complete the evaluation tasks in a group they know well.

> - this unit is not divided into six sessions, but into two parts, followed by a concluding celebration. Part One looks back over the programme, and to help in the process of evaluation and assessment, there is a set task; Part Two looks to the future, and to aid the reflection and discussion there are a further five set tasks. Be sure to allow plenty of time for each task.

PART ONE
EVALUATING THE PROGRAMME

TASK 1

The aim of this Part is to assess and evaluate the programme and the individual and group responses to it. To assist this, there is a photocopiable questionnaire in the worksheets. The first stage is that the students and group leaders each fill in one of these.

Only when there has been enough time for this personal reflection, move on to the group discussion that is suggested.

Personal thoughts on the programme (1)

Have you enjoyed following this programme? **YES/NO**
What was it that you did/that you didn't enjoy about the programme?

Which of the Units did you find most helpful?
Why do you think this was?

Which of the Units did you find least helpful?
Why do you think this was?

Did you find that you were listened to? That your views were taken seriously?

How easy or how difficult did you find it to speak out?

How easy or how difficult did you find it to take part in the small group activities?

From SEARCH FOR MEANING, published by Geoffrey Chapman, © Judith Russi SSMN 1990.

Personal thoughts on the programme (2)

Have your views about religion and its place in your life changed during the programme? **YES/NO**
If so, say how./If not, say why not.

Were there any moments during the programme when you felt angry?

Out of all the experiences the programme has offered you, which one would you rate as best; and why?

Please write here any advice you would like to offer your group leader about the programme and the way in which it was run.

Is there a topic you feel the programme should have covered, but didn't? What is it, and how might it be included?

Would you like to continue with some form of adult religious education in the future? **YES/NO**
If Yes, what sort of programme and topics? If No, why not?

From SEARCH FOR MEANING, published by Geoffrey Chapman. © Judith Russi SSMN 1990.
Multiple copies may be made only by the institution which has purchased a master set.

PART TWO
LOOKING TO THE FUTURE

The aim of this Part is to examine the possible responses that are before us at this moment in our lives.

Over the past months you have explored together many different aspects of life and the relationship between religion and life. Regardless of how we would now define our religious commitment, we are faced with several potential responsibilities, which we must take seriously.

Throughout the discussion, place due emphasis on the fact that each individual is being invited to make his or her own decision: there are no universally right and wrong answers, there are only answers which are 'right for me'. But while the decision is theirs, they should be aware that their decision will have consequences beyond themselves. Use a blackboard or a flip-chart to summarize the responses from the group.

Using and developing our gifts and talents:
- where are we going to direct our energy?
- what are our priorities?
- what are the things that are important for happiness in life?
- what type of work might we undertake?
- given a free choice, what kind of work would we want?
- do people have a mission in your life? do I?

Relationships:
- how do we really treat people?
- how much does the happiness of others matter to us?
- what about marriage and family?
- how seriously do we take these?

Leisure and recreation:
- how do these rate in my priorities?
- what responsibilities might we have here?

Meaning of life:
- how do we feel about making sense of life?
- do we have a responsibility to go on searching for the meaning of life?

- to what extent does God have a place in our life?

- can we ever say we know all we need to know about God?

THE CHURCH NEEDS YOU!

In the unit on community we looked at the phenomenon of basic Christian communities, and their potential for renewing local parish/church life. We return now to the idea of community, but with a particular emphasis now on the role of the individual.

We have discovered together that each of us is called to proclaim the Good News in a unique way, however small; that God has a vocation, a calling, for each one of us.

Regrettably, many people, especially young people, find it difficult to be attached to parish/church life in any fulfilling way. Their response is as evident as it is inevitable. They opt out, and look for other means of channelling their energy; they find other, more sustaining, means of support.

The challenge to us is to think through how we might be part of a process of renewal. Remember what we are interested in is renewal, not resuscitation! The latter is easier, often more attractive - but short-lived.

True renewal only happens when individuals understand, and accept, that their life has to change; and that they implement the change. Just as a family needs to work at staying together, at getting on with each other. This is not achieved by ignoring problems, but by laying problems and conflicts out in the open for all to face together, and to overcome.

The Church has long been afraid of conflict and disagreement. However, if our parishes are to be communities, then they must be places where we lay aside our misguided sense of loyalty and privatism, to replace it by shared common life. Not that every personal situation has to become everyone's concern, but rather the overall attitude of the parish should be one of caring for our brothers and sisters in Christ. For too long we have been happy with the vocabulary of 'community', but seldom if ever put it into practice. Actions speak louder than words. Our professed Christian witness is empty unless we ourselves live it.

Renewal begins when any individual anywhere takes his/her vocation, his/her ministry seriously; in fact, when they take themselves seriously. That is, when someone looks at the talents he/she has, and plans to use them for his/her own fulfilment and the building up of others. One thing is certain, everyone has a role to play.

The young adult population within the Church is potentially very powerful. No society, least of all the parish, can afford to lose the energy, enthusiasm and vision of the future that the young possess.

In this spirit, work through Tasks 2-6.

FINAL CELEBRATION

Hopefully, the students will feel that the programme should conclude with some form of celebration. Entrust the decision making and planning to them as much as possible.

Leave it to them to decide whether it happens during time allocated to the programme, or at a separate time.

They need to decide the most suitable venue.

They need to think what form the celebration should take, for example:

- a meal together;
- a meal together, with elements of prayer and thanksgiving;
- a party;
- a eucharist followed by a party/meal together.

Ensure that everyone has some part in the planning and the preparation.

CONCLUDING UNIT
Task 2

With one person from the group:

Share what you consider to be your strongest points, gifts, talents . . .

With the same person, discuss, honestly, what you think the next few years might hold for you.
Do you each think that what you expect to happen will help you to be fulfilled as a person?

Discuss the following together in groups:

What are the criteria you now use in choosing your friends?

Have these criteria changed since you were in your lower teens?

If so, how have they changed?

What do you think we mean when we talk about 'responsible relationships' in life?

Do you think that such relationships are easy, or possible in today's society?

Some people say that leisure activities (e.g. football, films/videos, discos, parties) seem to be becoming increasingly less creative, and increasingly mindless and violent?
Do you agree? Is this true?
Or is it just an unfair portrayal by the media?

You see a group of young teenagers causing trouble.

Would you do anything to stop them?

Either way, give your reasons.

TASK 3

ROLE PLAY
In groups of four:
Three of you are invited to
the fourth's house to watch
a video.
It turns out to be a
pornographic video.
One of you thinks it's funny;
a second pretends they've
seen it before, and fakes
boredom;
the third wants it turned off,
wants to see something better.

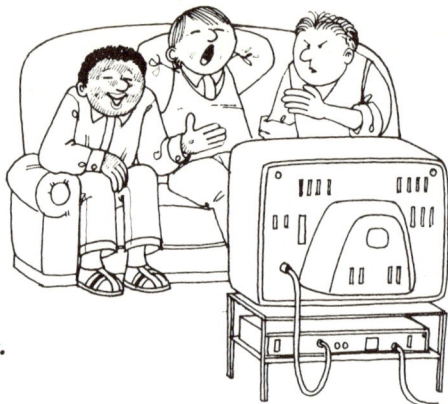

Act out the scenario.
How does it end?

Share your role play, or its conclusion, with the bigger group.

TASK 4

Spend a few minutes reflecting on the following question,
then write down your response:

At the moment, how far do you feel you should go
in searching for the meaning of life;
in searching for God in your life?

TASK 5

Arrange a meeting with members of your parish who are responsible for the various activities to come and share with you:
- how they see the parish;
- how they would define the role of the parish;
- how well they feel the parish is meeting the needs of its members.

Through discussion with them, build up a picture of the parish.
In particular,
- what is being done in the parish to develop the ministry of the laity?
- who is responsible for it?
- are the young people in the parish given the opportunity
to contribute in a creative and positive way?
- are the young people given any true responsibility in the parish?

Organise a parish survey.
Design questions that will elicit what people really feel about the parish,
and what they would like it to offer in the future.
Aim to reach a cross-section of the parishioners.

Collate your findings and present them to the parish council,
to the parish priest, to the bishop.
Don't forget to ask for a reply.

DEC
The
is in
No
and,
This

Pare
that
You
Ther
but

Disc

Wha

Do y
Wha

How

CO

The

Writ
com
Thes

Once
state